The ASVAB Tutor's Word Knowledge & Paragraph Comprehension Study Guide
by
Julie A. Hyers

The ASVAB Tutor's Word Knowledge and Paragraph Comprehension Study Guide
Julie A. Hyers © 2020

The Word Knowledge section of the ASVAB consists of vocabulary questions.

The book consists of vocabulary tips, common vocabulary words, Latin and Greek roots, prefixes, and suffixes.

Vocabulary Words

500+ vocabulary words are given and are broken up into 3 categories: Very Common List, Common List, and Useful List.

Roots, Prefixes and Suffixes
- Charts of Latin and Greek Word Roots with Meanings and Examples
- Chart of Prefixes with Meanings and Examples
- Chart of Suffixes with Meanings and Examples

In writing the book, research was done on the most common words used on the ASVAB.

The Very Common ASVAB Vocabulary Word List should be reviewed <u>first</u>
The list consists of 76 ASVAB vocabulary words. The words appeared <u>most</u> frequently in a wide variety of ASVAB study guides.

- 76 Very Common ASVAB words
- 76 Sentences with Context Clues for Very Common ASVAB Words
- 76 Videos for the Very Common ASVAB Words (online access)

The Common ASVAB Vocabulary Word List should be reviewed <u>second</u>.
The list consists of 188 ASVAB Vocabulary Words. The words appeared <u>frequently</u> in the ASVAB study guides but not as frequently as the Very Common List.

- 188 Common ASVAB Words
- 188 Sentences with Context Clues for Common ASVAB Words
- 188 Videos for the Common ASVAB Words (online access)

The Useful ASVAB Vocabulary Word List should be reviewed <u>third</u>.
The list consists of 247 Useful ASVAB Vocabulary Words that <u>commonly</u> appear in study guides. The words do not appear as frequently as the Common List.

- 247 Useful ASVAB Words
- 247 Sentences with Context Clues for Useful ASVAB Words
- 247 Videos for the Useful ASVAB Words (online access)

Roots, Prefixes and Suffixes
- Charts of Latin and Greek Word Roots with Meanings and Examples
- Chart of Prefixes with Meanings and Examples
- Chart of Suffixes with Meanings and Examples

Paragraph Comprehension Section

The Paragraph Comprehension section of the ASVAB consists of reading passages and questions based on the passages. The book consists of tips for reading passages and answering multiple-choice questions related to the passages.

Paragraph Comprehension includes different types of questions:
- Main Idea
- Detail
- Vocabulary
- Sequence
- Inference
- Cause and Effect
- Author's Tone
- Author's Purpose

The book consists of:

- Paragraph Comprehension Tips
- Introduction to Various Types of Paragraph Comprehension Questions
- Tips on Answering Different Types of Paragraph Comprehension Questions
- Reading Passages with Multiple-Choice Questions
- Answer Key and Explanations for the Answers

    Passages in this packet were taken from www.gutenberg.org
    The passages include different genres of literature including: nonfiction, fiction, editorials, folklore, myths, poetry, letters, and essays.

*Not responsible for typographical errors.

Table of Contents

ASVAB Vocabulary 500+ Words To Review

A

Abandon - to give up completely, to desert, to leave

Abate - to become less

Abdicate - to give up or surrender responsibility

Abet - to help

Abhor - to hate

Abhorrence - feeling of hating something or being disgusted by something

Abolish - to do away with

Abort - to cut short

Abridge - to shorten

Abscond - to leave quickly and secretly

Abstain - to voluntarily do without, to refrain from

Acclaim - approval

Accost - to approach and speak to in a bold way

Acumen - sharpness of mind

Acute - sharp, severe

Adamant - inflexible

Adept - skilled

Adequate - enough for what is required, sufficient

Adhere - to stick to a surface or to believe in and follow the practices of

Adjourn - to close a meeting for a time

Adroit - skillful

Adversary - opponent, foe, enemy

Advocate - one who speaks or writes in support of another

Aesthetic - having to do with beauty

Agile - able to move quickly and easily

Agitate - to make someone nervous or troubled

Allude - to refer to indirectly, hint at

Aloof - cool and reserved, distant

Ambidextrous - equally skilled in using both hands

Ambiguous - not clear in meaning, vague

Amenable - agreeable or willing to be influenced or persuaded

Amicable - friendly, peaceful

5

Amity - peaceful or friendly relations
Anomaly - abnormality
Apathy - lack of emotion
Appease - to pacify or satisfy by giving into the demands of
Apt - quick to learn
Aquatic - growing or living in the water
Ardent - passionate, burning
Arrogant - full of pride
Articulate - speaking clearly
Assert - to state a fact or belief confidently or forcefully
Assess - to set a value on
Astute - clever or wise
Attain - to gain
Atypical - abnormal
Augment - to increase or improve
Austere - severe
Authentic - genuine, real
Auxiliary - helping

B
Baffle - to completely confuse
Banal - lacking in originality, obvious and boring
Barred - not allowed
Barren - fruitless, unproductive, infertile
Belie - to disguise or misrepresent
Belligerent - warlike, ready to fight
Benevolent - kind or charitable
Bland - mild, also meaning lacking in flavor
Blatant - outright
Blemish - a flaw or defect
Boggy - wet, soggy (ground)
Bogus - not genuine, false
Boycott - to withdraw from relations with a country, organization, or person as a punishment or
          protest
Brevity - briefness
Brusque - rudely brief

C
Calligraphy - fancy handwriting
Candid - very honest and open
Capricious - having sudden, impulsive thinking or actions
Carcass - dead body of an animal
Cease - to stop
Chaos - extreme confusion or disorder
Chide - to scold or express disapproval of
Chronic - happening for a long time

Clandestine - secret or hidden
Coerce - to force
Cogent - convincing to the point
Coherent - logical and consistent, understandable
Collaborate - to work together
Colleague - a worker in the same profession
Comparable - able to be likened or compared to another
Compatible - able to get along well together
Competent - capable or adequate
Complacent - self-satisfied
Compose - to make up or create
Compromise - an agreement that is reached by each side giving up something each one wanted
Concede - to give in, to surrender or yield
Concept - idea or thought
Concise - brief and to the point
Conduct - behavior
Confidential - meant to be kept secret
Conscientious - wishing to do what is right, especially to do one's work well
Consequence - the result or effect
Consume - to use up
Contaminate - to make corrupt or pollute
Contempt - the feeling one has toward someone they view as worthless
Corrugated - grooved
Covert - hidden or disguised
Credible - believable
Credulous - believing anything
Creed - a statement of religious belief
Culpable - deserving blame
Cumbersome - burdensome, difficult to carry
Cursory - done quickly on the surface
Curt - rudely brief
Curtail - to shorten or reduce

D
Dearth - scarcity or lack
Debilitate - to make weak
Debonair - confident, stylish, charming
Deceive - to mislead or trick someone
Decimate - to destroy or kill a large part of
Decrepit - broken down or worn out by old age
Deft - skilled
Defunct - dead or extinct
Defy - to oppose something
Delete - to take out, to cross out
Demolish - to destroy
Demote - to reduce to a lower rank

Deplete - to use up
Deplore - to be sorry about or to disapprove
Deprive - to take away from forcibly
Destitute/Destitution - extreme poverty
Detest - to hate
Detrimental - causing damage
Deviation - a departing from the accepted or normal standard
Diffident - shy
Digress - to wander from the subject in talking or writing
Diminish - to make or become smaller in size
Disburse - to pay out
Discard - to get rid of
Discern - to figure out or recognize
Disclose - to reveal
Disdain - to look down upon someone or despise him or her
Dismal - dark and gloomy
Dismay - disappointment
Dispel - to scatter or drive away
Disperse - to break up or scatter
Disrupt - to disturb or interrupt
Diverge - to go in different directions
Diverse - different, varied
Divert - to distract
Divulge - to reveal
Docile - easy to discipline, submissive
Domicile - home, residence
Dormant - inactive or sleeping state
Dubious - hesitating or doubting
Durable - something that lasts a long time, even with frequent use
Dwindle - to keep becoming smaller or less, to diminish or shrink

E
Eccentric - odd, unusual
Eclectic - selected from various sources
Economical - not wasting money, thrifty
Edible - able to be eaten
Efface - to erase
Eject - to remove
Elate - to make happy
Elusive - difficult to find, catch, or achieve
Empathy - the ability to share in another's emotions, thoughts, or feelings
Enable - to make able or possible
Enhance - to make greater or better
Enlightened - free from ignorance or prejudice
Entitle - to give a title or a right or claim to something
Equivocal - having two or more meanings, purposely unclear

Eulogy - positive speech about someone usually at a funeral
Evaluate - to find out the value of something
Evasive - seeking to avoid or escape by deceit or cleverness
Evoke - to call forth
Expel - to remove by force
Exploit - to use someone or something for profit
Extraneous - irrelevant or unrelated to the topic at hand

F
Facetious - joking especially at an inappropriate time
Fallacious - based on a mistaken belief
Famished - hungry or starving
Feasible - capable of being done, possible
Feigned - faked
Feud - fight
Fickle - changeable, unstable, capricious
Fidget - restless or nervous movement
Flaunt - to show off
Fluorescent - bright light
Forfeit - to lose or have taken away
Forlorn - very sad or hopeless
Fortuitous - happening by chance, lucky
Frail - weak
Fraudulent - trickery, deceit
Frugal - not wasteful, being very careful with money, thrifty
Fundamental - forming a foundation or basis
Futile - useless

G
Genesis - origin or beginning
Germane - relevant, important
Ghastly - horrible, frightful
Glut - too much of something, excess
Gracious - having or showing kindness, courtesy or charm
Grating - irritating sound
Gratis - free
Gregarious - sociable, enjoying company of others
Grievance - a complaint against something viewed as wrong
Grievous - causing grief or sorrow
Grim - something unpleasant, depressing, or difficult to accept
Gross - very bad
Grotesque - distorted appearance
Gruesome - horrible or disgusting
Guile - sly, crafty, tricky
Gullible - easily fooled
Guttural - harsh sound from deep in the throat

H

Hale - healthy
Haphazard - random
Hardy - strong, bold
Harass - to make repeated attacks on someone
Haughty - arrogant
Hectic - full of activity, very busy, fast
Hilarious - funny
Hinder - to keep back, to stop
Hoax - a trick or fraud
Hoist - to lift
Homogenous - made up of similar parts
Horrendous - horrible
Hostile - aggressive
Humid - damp, wet
Humorous - funny

I

Illicit - illegal
Illusion - a false idea
Immaculate - very clean
Immune - protected from against something harmful
Impair - to weaken
Impartial - fair, without bias
Impeccable - flawless, without error
Imperative - necessary, urgent
Impertinent - rude
Impetuous - acting with little thought, impulsive
Imply - to hint or suggest
Impressive - bringing about admiration of others
Impromptu - done without preparation
Impudent - bold or fearless
Incendiary - able to cause a fire or explosion
Inception - beginning or start
Incinerate - to burn
Inclement - rough or stormy
Incognito - in disguise
Incoherent - unable to be understood
Indelible - unable to be erased
Indifferent - neutral, unconcerned
Indigenous - existing or growing naturally in a region or country
Indigent - poor, humble
Indispensable - absolutely needed
Induct - to admit someone to a position or organization
Inept - unfit or unskilled
Inertia - an object at rest remains at rest, while an object in motion remains in motion

Infallible - unable to make mistakes
Inferior - lower in order, status, or rank
Infinite - without limits, endless
Infinitesimal - very small
Inflexible - not flexible, stiff, rigid
Ingenious - clever
Ingenuous - simple
Inhabit - to live in
Inherent - existing in someone naturally
Initiate - to bring into practice or use
Innate - inborn
Innocuous - harmless
Innovation - the process of introducing new methods
Insipid - uninteresting or boring
Instill - to put into
Instinct - a natural or inborn tendency to behave a certain way
Integrity - completeness or honesty
Intermittent - stopping and starting at intervals
Intuition - the ability to acquire knowledge without proof or evidence
Irate - extremely angry
Itinerary - a detailed plan for a journey

J
Jargon - specialized vocabulary relating to a profession
Jeopardy - in danger
Jetty - a wall built to protect a harbor
Jubilant - joyful
Judicious - fair

K
Knead - to fold, press or mold dough, clay, etc.

L
Lament - to feel or express deep sorrow, to mourn
Latent - hidden
Laudable - praiseworthy
Legible - able to be read
Leisurely - done without haste in a slow or unhurried manner
Lethal - deadly
Lethargic - drowsy, sluggish
Levelheaded - sensible
Levity - lightheartedness
Limber - flexible
Listless - lifeless
Lithe - flexible
Loathe - to feel intense dislike or hatred

Lofty - very high, grand
Lucid - clear, easily understood
Lucrative - producing wealth, profitable
Luminous - glowing or shining a bright light

M
Magnitude - greatness in size or extent
Majestic - grand, fancy
Malady - illness
Malicious - evil
Malign - to speak badly about someone
Malignant - cancerous
Malleable - able to be hammered or changed into different shapes without breaking
Mammoth - very large
Manual - done by hand
Massive - very large
Meager - small, inadequate amount
Meander - to wander
Mediocre - ordinary, average
Memento - a souvenir, something to help remember a time or place
Mend - to repair or make better
Mercenary - working for money only
Meritorious - deserving reward or praise
Meticulous - very exact about details
Militant - aggressive, ready to fight
Minute - very small
Misnomer - a wrong name
Mitigate - to make less severe
Momentous - very important
Morose - gloomy
Motivation - the reason one has for acting or behaving in a certain way
Mundane - worldly, commonplace, ordinary

N
Naïve - gullible, quick to believe what one is told
Nascent - beginning to form or develop
Neglectful - failing to give proper care to something or someone, careless, inattentive
Negligence/Negligent - careless, failing to do the right thing
Nonchalant - casually calm or relaxed
Notary - an official who can certify documents
Notify - to inform
Notorious - famous in a bad way
Novice - a beginner
Noxious - harmful
Nullify/Null - to make invalid/invalid

O

Objective - fair
Obligation - a duty or commitment
Obliterated - destroyed
Oblivious - not aware of or concerned about what is happening around oneself
Obscure - dark or not easily seen
Obsequious - having an excessive willingness to serve others
Obsess - to haunt or trouble the mind
Obsolete - no longer in use, out of date
Obstinate - stubborn
Obtuse - slow to understand
Offish - unfriendly
Omit - to leave out
Omnipotent - having unlimited power or authority, all-powerful
Onus - burden
Opportune - good timing
Optimum - best or most favorable condition
Opulent - very wealthy
Origin - beginning
Ostentatious - showy display, flashy
Ostracize - to exclude someone from a group

P

Pacify - to soothe, calm
Panoramic - a wide view in all directions
Paradox - a statement that seems contradictory but is true
Passive - accepting or allowing what happens or what others do without active response
Peculiar - odd, strange
Pensive - thoughtful or reflective
Perpetual - lasting forever
Persist - to refuse to give up
Petty - unimportant, small, trivial
Petulance - the quality of being easily annoyed by minor things, like a bad-tempered child
Picayune - very small, unimportant
Placid - calm, quiet
Plausible - believable
Plethora - overabundance, excess
Poignant - emotionally moving
Posthumous - happening after one's death
Potent - powerful
Potential - ability
Pragmatic - practical
Precarious - risky
Precocious - mature at an early age
Predator - an animal that lives by killing and eating other animals or a person who seeks to use others to control them

Predicament - unpleasant or embarrassing situation
Prejudiced - having an unfair dislike of a person or group beforehand
Premature - arriving before the proper or usual time, too early
Prestige - association with high achievement or influence
Primary - first in order
Principal - first in rank or importance
Proclaim - to announce officially
Procrastinate - to put off doing until later, delay
Prodigious - very large in size, force or extent, enormous
Profane - disrespect or bad language, swearing
Profess - to claim to believe something
Proficient - skilled
Profound - having great knowledge or insight
Profusely - abundantly, in large amounts
Prohibit - to forbid or prevent
Prolong - to lengthen in time or space
Promote - to raise to a higher position or rank
Prompt - on time
Prosperous - successful, wealthy
Protest - to express disapproval
Proximity - nearness
Prudent - acting wisely showing care and thought for the future
Punctuality - being on time or prompt

Q
Quandary - to be in an uncertain situation, a dilemma
Quarrel - a dispute or a fight
Quell - to quiet
Quench - to put out a fire, to satisfy one's thirst
Query - question, inquiry

R
Rampant - widespread
Rancor - bitterness or resentfulness
Random - purposeless, happening by chance
Ravage - to cause destruction or ruin
Recede - to move or go backward
Recur - to happen repeatedly
Redundant - exceeding what is needed
Refrain - to hold back, to keep oneself from doing something
Regimen - a system to improve one's health
Reiterate - to say or do again repeatedly
Relevant - relating to the matter at hand, important
Relinquish - to give up
Reluctant - unwilling
Repress - to hold back, restrain

Requisite - required or necessary
Rescind - to cancel
Resent - to feel sorrow or show displeasure or hurt, bitterness
Reserve - to save for later
Restrict - to keep within limits
Resume - to continue after interruption
Retain - to continue to have or keep possession of
Retaliate/Retaliation - to seek revenge
Reticent - unwilling to speak, quiet
Retroactive - having an effect on things that are already past
Revive - to bring back to life
Rodent - small mammal that gnaws with their teeth, ex: rats, mice
Rudiments/Rudimentary - basic principles
Rue - to feel regret or be sorry for
Ruminate - to think deeply about something

S
Salient - most noticeable or important
Satchel - a small bag
Satiate - to provide with more than enough, glut
Savory - tasty
Scant - inadequate, not enough
Scrappy - ready to fight
Scorn - the feeling or belief that someone or something is worthless
Scrupulous - diligent, thorough, and extremely attentive to details
Secure - free from danger, safe
Sentimental - showing feelings of tenderness, sadness, or remembrance of the past
Shrine - a religious site
Slander - to speak falsely about another person to ruin their reputation
Slate - to arrange for something to happen
Slender - thin
Slovenly - untidy or sloppy
Solemn - serious
Sophisticated - knowledgeable of the world, not simple
Sordid - dirty or wretched
Spiritual - relating to the soul or religion
Spiteful - cruel, mean, vengeful
Sporadic - happening at random
Squalid - unclean or wretched
Stalwart - strong, sturdy
Steadfast - firm, fixed, or constant
Stealthy - behaving in a cautious way so not to be seen or heard
Strident - harsh-sounding, shrill
Sturdy - strong
Subordinate - below another in rank or importance
Substantial - of considerable importance, size, or worth

Subtle - not obvious
Succinct - clear and brief
Sufficient - as much as is needed, enough
Superficial - existing or occurring on the surface
Superfluous - excessive or unnecessary
Superior - higher in order, rank, etc.
Supplement - something added to make up for lack
Surfeit - an excessive amount of something, too much
Surmount - to overcome a challenge
Suspend - to stop temporarily
Sustain - to keep in existence, to maintain
Sympathetic - feeling, showing, or expressing pity or sorrow for someone else's misfortunes

T
Tactful/Tact - being able to say the right thing without offending someone
Tangible - something you can touch
Taut - tightly stretched
Tedious - long, slow or tiresome
Tenacious/Tenacity - one who does not give up/persistent
Terminate - to end or stop
Tentative - when something is done but is not final
Terse - brief, short
Thrift - to be careful with money, economical
Timid - shy
Transition - passing from one condition or place to another, a change
Transpose - to change the order of
Turmoil - great confusion or uncertainty

U
Unanimous - all agreeing
Unethical - not morally correct, morally wrong
Unison - action or speech done all at the same time
Unwieldy - hard to carry because of large size
Utilize - to use

V
Vacant - empty
Vagrant - a person who travels from place to place and begs to make a living
Vague - unclear
Vain - producing no effect, useless; also means having a high opinion of one's appearance
Valid - reasonable or logical; legally or officially acceptable
Vapid - tasteless, dull
Variable - changeable
Verify - to prove to be true
Vestibule - small entrance or hall
Vex - to annoy

Vicious - mean or evil
Victor - winner
Vigilant - staying watchful and alert to danger
Vilify - abusive language
Vindictive - seeking revenge
Vital - essential to life
Vivid - lively or colorful
Vociferous - noisy
Volatile - changeable, threatening to break out in violence

W

Warily - cautiously or carefully
Wary - cautious or careful
Wheeze - difficult breathing with a whistling sound
Whim - a sudden, passing idea
Wince - to shrink back in pain
Witty - funny in a clever way

Z

Zeal/Zealous/Zealot - to show enthusiasm or passion
Zest - enthusiasm or passion

Prefix	Meaning	Example
a-, an-	not, without	amorphous
ab-, a-, abs-,	apart, away from	absent
ad-, a-, ac-, af-, ag-	near to, toward	adjoin
ambi-, amphi-	both	amphibian
ante-	before	antechamber
anti-	against	antiwar
arch-	highest, supreme	archenemy
auto-	self	autobiography
be-	completely, covered with	befriend
bene-	good, well	benevolent
circum-	around	circumvent
co-, col-, con-, cor-	together, with	collaborate
com-	bring together	companion
contra-	against	contradict
counter-	opposite, against	counteract
de-	away from, down, undoing	defrost
dia-, di-	across, through	diameter
dis-	not	disbelief
dis-, di-, dif-	apart, away from	diverge
en-, em-	to cover, into	embrace
epi-, ep-, eph-	among, besides, upon	epicenter
eu-	well	eulogy
ex-	out, former	exclude
exo-	outside	exoskeleton
extra-	outside, beyond	extraterrestrial
fore-	before	foremost
hetero-	different	heterogenous
homo	same	homogenous
hyper-	above, excessive	hyperactive
hypo-	below, under	hypoactive
icon-, icono-	image	iconoclast
il-, in-, ir-, im-	not	illogical
in-	not	insensitive
in-	into	inborn
infra-	below, beneath	infrared
inter-	between	interpersonal
intra-	within	intramural
juxta-	near, next to	juxtapose
macro-	large, long	macrobiotic
mal-	bad, evil, ill	malediction
mega-	large, powerful	megaphone
meta-	changed, with, beyond	metaphysics
micro-	enlarges or very small	microphone
mid-	middle	midpoint

mini-	small	miniscule
mis-	wrong	misinterpret
multi-	much, many	multidimensional
neo-	new	neonatal
non-	not	nonessential
ob-, oc-, of-, op-	against, toward, to	obstruction
ortho-	correct, straight	orthopedic
out-	from, beyond	outshine
over-	above, too much	overweight
paleo-	old, ancient	paleolithic
pan-	all	pandemic
para-	beside	parallel
peri-	around, near	perimeter
poly-	many	polygon
post-	after, behind	postpone
pre-	before	preread
pro-	before, in favor of	promote
pseudo-	false	pseudonym
re-	again	rewrite
retro-	backward	retroactive
se-	apart	secede
sub-, suc-, suf-, sug-, sum-, sup-, sur-, sus-,	below, under, nearly, lower	submerge
subter-	beneath, secretly	subterfuge
super-	above, over	superintendent
supra-	above, beyond	supraorbital
syn-, syl-, sym-, sys-	together, with	synchronized
tele-	from a distance	telecommunications
therm-	heat	thermometer
tor-	twist	contortionist
trans-	across	transcontinental
twi-	two	twice
ultra-	beyond	ultraviolet
un-	not	unnecessary
under-	below	underneath
up-	greater, higher, better	uptown
vert-, verse	change	convert
with-	against, back	withstand

Prefix Related to Numbers	Meaning	Example
uni-	one	unicycle
mono-	one	monopoly
bi-	two	bilateral
di-	two	dichotomy
tri-	three	triped
quad-	four	quadrilateral
semi-	half	semicircle
hemi-	half	hemisphere
deca-	ten	decathlon
centi-	hundred, hundredth	century
mille-	thousand, thousandth	millennium
kilo-	thousand	kilogram

Root Word	Meaning	Example
act	do	activate
aero	air	aerodynamics
ambu	walk	ambulate
annu, annui	year	annual
anthro, anthrop	man, human	anthropology
aster, ast	star	asteroid
audi	hear	audible
auto	self	automated
bene	good, well	beneficial
bibl, biblio	book	bibliography
bio	life	biological
brev	short	abbreviate
capit	head	capital
card, cord, cour	heart	cardiology
carn	flesh	carnivore
cas	fall	cascade
ced, cede	go, yield	recede
chrom	color	monochromatic
chron, chrono	time	chronological
cid, cide	killing	pesticide
cis	cut	incision
claim	shout, cry out	proclaim
clud, clude	close	conclude
cogn	know	cognizant
cor	heart	coronary
crat	rule	autocrat
cred	believe	credible
culp	blame	culpable
curr	run	current
dem	people	democracy
dic, dict	speak	dictate
do, don	give	donation
domin	rule	dominate
dorm	sleep	dormant
duc, duct	lead, make	conduct
equ, equi	equal, same	equilateral
fac, fact	make	manufacture
fer	carry	transfer
fin	end	finalize
flect	bend	inflection
flu, fluc	flow	influx
form	shape	formation
fract	break	fracture

frater	brother	fraternity
fuge	flee	refugee
gen	birth	generation
geo	earth	geology
gram	written, drawn	telegram
graph	write	graphics
gress	walk	transgress
jec, ject	throw	projectile
junct	join	juncture
jur, jus	law	justice
labor	work	laborious
liber	free	liberation
lingue	language, tongue	bilingual
litera	letter	literary
lith	stone	lithography
loc	place	location
log, logue, logy	word, thought	monologue
lum, luc, lumen	light	illuminate
mal	bad, evil	malicious
man, manu	hand	manuscript
mand, mend	order	command
mar	sea	maritime
mater	mother	maternal
ment	mind	mental
meter, metr	measure	metric
mit	send	transmit
morph	form	morphology
mort	die	mortality
mot	move	motility
nom	name	nomenclature
norm	rule	abnormal
nov	new	novice
omni	all	omnipotent
op, oper	work	operation
par	equal	parity
pater	father	paternity
path, pathy	feeling	empathy
ped	child	pediatrician
ped, pod	foot	podiatry
pend	hanging	pendulum
phil, philo	love	philosophy
phobe, phobia	fear	agoraphobia
phon	sound	phonics
port	carry	transport
phys	body, nature	physical

press	squeeze	compression
psych	body, nature	psychological
pug, pugn	fight	pugnacious
rupt	break	rupture
sci	know	conscience
scrib, script	write	scribe
sect	cut	resection
sens, sent	feel	sentimental
sol	alone	solitary
soph	wise	sophomore
spect	look	retrospect
stro, stru, struct	build	construct
temp	time	temporal
tele	far away	televise
terr	earth	territory
tract	pull	traction
vac	empty	vacate
vad	go	evade
ven, vent	come	adventure
verb	word	verbose
vert	turn	revert
vid, vis	see	visual
vict	conquer	victory
voc, vok	call, voice	evoke
vol, volv	turn, roll	revolution

Suffix	Meaning	Example
-able, -ible	able	livable
-ade	result	serenade
-age	act of	shrinkage
-al	pertaining to	seasonal
-ance, -ence	an action	deviance
-ant	one who performs an act	defendant
-archy	rule, government	anarchy
-ate	cause, make	condensate
-ation	action, process	exploration
-biosis	life	symbiosis
-chrome	color	monochrome
-cide, -cidal	killer or destroyer	insecticide
-clasm, -clysm	breaker, destroyer	cataclasm
-derm	skin	hypodermic
-en	made from	wooden
-er,-or, -ess, -ist	one who	empress
-escence, -escent	becoming	effervescent
-fer	to produce	conifer
-ful	full of	grateful
-fy, -ify	to make or cause	glorify
-gamy	marriage	polygamy
-gnosis	knowledge	prognosis
-gram, -graph, -graphy	writing	biography
-hedral, -hedron	sided	polyhedron
-iatrics, -iatry	medical treatment	pediatrics
-ic	relating to, like	comic
-ical	possessing a quality of	theatrical
-ion	result of, act of	infusion
-ish	like, similar	childish
-ism, -istic	characteristic of	enthusiastic
-ist	one who characterizes	chemist
-itis, -is	inflammation	arthritis
-ity	quality of	amity
-ize, -ise	to cause to be, to become	emphasize
-latry	worship of	idolatry
-less	without	heedless
-let	small one	piglet
-lith	stone	monolith
-logue, -log	speech, word	dialogue
-machy	battle, fight	logomachy
-man	relating to humans	chairman
-mania, -maniac	excessive like of, psychosis	pyromania
-ment	act of	abandonment
-morphic, -morphous	shape	amorphous

-ness	possessing a quality of	kindness
-nomy	science, law of	astronomy
-oid	resembling, like	asteroid
-ous	full of, having	courteous
-pathy	suffering, disease	empathy
-phobe, phobia	fear of	arachnophobia
-phone, -phony	sound	cacophony
-plasm	matter	neoplasm
-saur	lizard	dinosaur
-scope	observation	microscope
-sect	cut, divided	dissect
-ty, -ity	state of being	levity
-vorous, -vore	eating	omnivore
-y	quality of	witty

Very Common ASVAB Vocabulary Review

List 1
Part 1

Very Common ASVAB Vocabulary Words

Abdicate to Authentic

1. Abdicate

The queen will give up her power when she will <u>abdicate</u> the throne to a new queen.

(Cat video) I will <u>abdicate</u> my role as king. I have decided to give up my power.

Definition:_____

_____

2. Abhorrence/Abhor

The act of abusing children is an <u>abhorrence.</u>
I <u>abhor</u> pedophiles.

(Cat video) People think I <u>abhor</u> dogs just because I am a cat, but I actually love dogs.

Definition:_____

_____

3. Abscond

The bank robber plans to <u>abscond</u> with all the money he stole so no one will find him.

(Cat video) It was my job to track down the bank robber who decided to <u>abscond</u> with all the money. He decided to run away and try to hide.

Definition:_____

_____

4. Accost

Renee was <u>accosted</u> by a man on the street that said, "Hey lady, what are you looking at?"

(Cat video) We are on the search for a suspect who decided to <u>accost</u> a woman. He came up to her, approached her in an alley and spoke to her in an aggressive way and frightened her.

Definition:_____

_____

5. Adept

Matthew is very <u>adept</u> in martial arts and just earned his black belt.

(Cat video) I am very <u>adept</u> at climbing. It's just one of the many things that I am skilled at.

Definition:_____

_____

6. Ardent

The president of the National Rifle Association is an <u>ardent</u> supporter of the right to possess a gun.

(Cat video) I am an <u>ardent</u> supporter of animal rights, and you may wonder what makes me so passionate about this. But you have to remember, I am an animal myself!

Definition:_____

_____

7. Arrogant

The <u>arrogant</u> man constantly bragged about his achievements.

(Cat video) People call me <u>arrogant</u>. They say I brag too much, but you know what I say, when you've got it, flaunt it.

Definition:_____

_____

8. Articulate

Sonia earned an A+ in her public speaking class since she is such an <u>articulate</u> speaker.

(Cat video) I am very <u>articulate</u> for a cat. I speak clearly at all times.

Definition:_____

_____

9. Augment

Louise decided to <u>augment</u> her income by taking on a second job.

(Cat video) I was told this outfit would <u>augment</u> my appearance. Do you think it improves how I look?

Definition:_____

_____

10. Authentic

Analisa bought an <u>authentic</u> leather bag because she did not like the fake leather ones she saw.

(Cat video) When people see me, they ask, "Is that an <u>authentic</u> cat?" I say, "This is as real as it gets. No filters needed here."

Definition:_____

_____

List 1
Part 2

Very Common ASVAB Vocabulary Words

Blatant to Digress

1. Blatant

The child told a <u>blatant</u> lie that he did not eat the chocolate cake even though he had icing all over his mouth.

(Cat video) When my owner asks me, "Cuddles, are you in my grocery bag again?" I say, "Nope." I tell a <u>blatant</u> lie. I know it is an outright and obvious lie, but I just can't help myself.

Definition:_____

_____

2. Blemish

Martin was upset about the <u>blemish</u> on his brand-new car after it was hit with a shopping cart in the parking lot.

(Cat video) I am wearing these glasses to try to hide a <u>blemish</u> on my face. I don't need anyone to see my flaws.

Definition:_____

_____

3. Brevity

The teacher reviewed for the test with <u>brevity</u>, and after 5 minutes she quickly moved on to the next topic.

(Cat video) I like to speak with <u>brevity</u>. I like to be brief and to the point in everything I say.

Definition:_____

_____

4. Brusque

Michael gave Jessica a <u>brusque</u> response to her question about his job interview, and she was surprised by his rude reaction.

(Cat video) My friend, Snuggles, gave me a <u>brusque</u> comment this morning. I said, "Hi Snuggles, how are you?", and he said, "Whatever." I just cannot believe how rudely brief he was with me today.

Definition:_____

_____

5. Cease

The soldier stopped shooting when the sergeant yelled, "<u>Cease</u> fire!"

(Cat video) I am not sure when the rain is going to <u>cease</u>, but when it does stop, I am going back outside.

Definition:_____

_____

6. Chide

The mother will <u>chide</u> her son for disobeying her rule of being home before dark.

(Cat video) I better get off the counter before my owner sees me and starts to <u>chide</u> me saying, "Cuddles, get off the counter! Cuddles, you are such a bad cat!" Oh brother!

Definition:_____

_____

7. Cumbersome

The refrigerator was <u>cumbersome</u> to move due to its size and weight.

(Cat video) This headscarf is so <u>cumbersome</u>. I really have a difficult time carrying it around on my head.

Definition:_____

_____

8. Cursory

The doctor performed a <u>cursory</u> examination on the patient, giving her a quick check up without an in-depth evaluation of her health.

(Cat video) The witness gave a <u>cursory</u> description of the suspect. Since the description was not very detailed, it will be difficult to identify the suspect.

Definition:_____

_____

9. Detest

The honest man <u>detests</u> a liar.

(Cat video) I really <u>detest</u> how this wig looks on me. Don't you hate it too?

Definition:_____

_____

10. Digress

The college professor tends to <u>digress</u> during his lectures, often starting on one topic and ending up on another.

(Cat video) Hello, all. It's me, Cuddles. Let me tell you a few things about myself. First of all, I am a cat, which you probably know. And oh, wait a minute. Oh, there goes a moth. Oh boy, I love to eat them. Hold on. Oh gee. I am sorry I decided to <u>digress</u>. It is hard for me sometimes to stay on topic, especially when a moth passes by.

Definition:_____

_____

31

List 1
Part 3

Very Common ASVAB Vocabulary Words

Disdain to Haughty

1. Disdain

Rodger worked hard in the company for 10 years to try to become manager, and he held <u>disdain</u> for the boss's son who was made manager after one week of working in the company.

(<u>Cat video</u>) I have a great amount of <u>disdain</u> for villains. I really look down on the bad guys, which is why I decided to become a superhero.

Definition:_____

_____

2. Domicile

Vanessa told me the address of her new <u>domicile</u> after she had moved.

(<u>Cat video</u>) Welcome to my <u>domicile</u>. This is the place that I call home.

Definition:_____

_____

3. Economical

Smaller cars tend to be more <u>economical</u> when it comes to their use of fuel.

(<u>Cat video</u>) I make <u>economical</u> choices when it comes to spending my money. I always make sure that I don't spent too much.

Definition:_____

_____

4. Flaunt

After losing 200 pounds, the woman was so excited to <u>flaunt</u> her new figure at her high school reunion in front of all who had bullied her in school.

(Cat video) How do you like my new car? I figured I might as well <u>flaunt</u> it. No sense in having a new car if you're not going to show it off!

Definition:_____

_____

5. Frail

The <u>frail</u> elderly woman broke a bone in her back when she tripped over a rock.

(Cat video) People think I am <u>frail</u> because I am small, but I'm actually not weak at all.

Definition:_____

_____

6. Frugal

Rosa was very <u>frugal</u> with her money, making sure to watch for sales, cut coupons, and return bottles for recycling.

(Cat video) I have always been very <u>frugal</u> with my money. I make sure I watch out for sales and cut coupons.

Definition:_____

_____

7. Ghastly

After being hospitalized for several weeks, Lou had a <u>ghastly</u> appearance.

(Cat video) I have a <u>ghastly</u> appearance while wearing this wig. It really looks horrible on me.

Definition:_____

_____

8. Grievous/Grievance

Finding out about the young child's serious illness was <u>grievous</u> news.

The women filed a <u>grievance</u> against their employer for unfair treatment.

(Cat video) I am planning to file a <u>grievance</u> against my stylist for sending me out in the world looking like this. Tomorrow morning, I am writing up a complaint.

Definition:_____

_____

9. Hale

The 100-year-old woman is still <u>hale</u> despite her age since her last medical checkup showed no major health issues.

(Cat video) I eat right, and I exercise, and I am still <u>hale</u>. It does prove that taking care of yourself makes you healthy.

Definition:_____

_____

10. Haughty

The <u>haughty</u> man considers himself better than everyone else**.**

(Cat video) Some might call me <u>haughty</u> because I look down on others, but I am out driving in my car while my friends are sleeping 16 hours a day. So, I have reason.

Definition:_____

_____

List 1
Part 4

Very Common ASVAB Vocabulary Words

Hilarious to Indigent

1. Hilarious

The comedian told hilarious jokes.

(Cat video) Why do cats make the worst storytellers? Because they only have one tale (tail). Haha! Am I hilarious or what? Boy, I sure am funny.

Definition:_____

_____

2. Hostile

The dog was hostile toward the intruders in trying to protect his owners.

(Cat video) People think I look hostile just because I have a lion's mane, but I am not aggressive at all.

Definition:_____

_____

3. Immaculate

Virginia had an immaculate house since she spent 5 hours every day cleaning it to make sure it was perfect.

(Cat video) My dress is immaculate. It is spotlessly clean.

Definition:_____

_____

4. Impair

Drinking alcohol can <u>impair</u> a person's ability to drive properly.

(Cat video) This costume <u>impairs</u> my ability to move. I am having a hard time getting around with this one on.

Definition:_____

_____

5. Imperative

Passing the ASVAB is an <u>imperative</u> part of joining the military because without passing it, people cannot enter.

(Cat video) Being physically fit is an <u>imperative</u> part of joining the military. So that means it is necessary to be in shape. So, drop and give me 20!

Definition:_____

_____

6. Impertinent

The 16-year-old girl was <u>impertinent</u> to her mother, showing little respect.

(Cat video) Hi Snuggles, how are you? What? You don't even answer me. I can't believe my best friend is so <u>impertinent</u>. How do I end up with a rude friend?

Definition:_____

_____

7. Impetuous

The <u>impetuous</u> child ran through the wet concrete without thinking.

(Cat video) People call me <u>impetuous</u>. They say I act without thinking. I guess they're right.

Definition:_____

_____

8. Incognito

Mr. Jones testified against the murderer and needed to spend the rest of his life <u>incognito</u> so no one would ever recognize him.

(Cat video) I am <u>incognito</u> as a college professor. No one will ever recognize me in this disguise.

Definition:_____

_____

9. Incoherent

The drunken man's speech was <u>incoherent</u> since no one could understand him.

All my animal friends are talking to me at the same time, and it's just so <u>incoherent</u>. I can't understand what anyone's saying.

Definition:_____

_____

10. Indigent

The boy came from an <u>indigent</u> family who could not afford to pay for his basic needs.

(Cat video) I came from an <u>indigent</u> background. I was born on the streets without much food. We were poor before I was adopted.

Definition:_____

_____

List 1
Part 5

Very Common ASVAB Vocabulary Words

Inflexible to Massive

1. Inflexible

The construction boss was very <u>inflexible</u> in his plans for the building despite all the setbacks he was experiencing.

(Cat video) My friend, Snuggles, is very <u>inflexible</u> in his plans. When he makes his mind up, no one can change it. He is just so rigid, stiff and not flexible.

Definition:_____

_____

2. Inhabit

Deer <u>inhabit</u> wooded areas.

(Cat video) Some animals live in the woods, but I <u>inhabit</u> a lovely camper.

Definition:_____

_____

3. Innate

The soccer star's son had an <u>innate</u> talent for playing soccer without ever having received lessons.

(Cat video) I have an <u>innate</u> ability to spot birds a mile away. It was just a gift I was born with.

Definition:_____

_____

4. Intermittent

Tuesday was an overcast day with <u>intermittent</u> rain that kept starting and stopping throughout the day.

(Cat video) I'm dressed for today's <u>intermittent</u> rain. It just keeps stopping and starting all day long.

Definition:_____

_____

5. Judicious

The teen made a <u>judicious</u> decision to not drink and drive.

(Cat video) As king, I have always been known for being <u>judicious</u>. The people appreciate me for my fairness.

Definition:_____

_____

6. Latent

Jan had a <u>latent</u> talent for singing that no one knew about until her mother heard her singing in the shower.

(Cat video) I have many <u>latent</u> talents. There are so many hidden talents I have that no one even knows about yet.

Definition:_____

_____

7. Listless

After taking the cold medicine, Reggie was <u>listless</u> and stayed in bed for the rest of the day.

(Cat video) I feel so <u>listless</u> today. I am just lying here with my lifeless body stretched across the bed.

Definition:_____

_____

8. Lofty

The 100-foot tall oak tree had such <u>lofty</u> branches.

The highly educated woman was very <u>lofty</u> in how she spoke to uneducated people.

(Cat video) I like to climb to <u>lofty</u> places. Are you impressed with how high I can climb?

Definition:_____

_____

9. Malign

Sometimes magazines <u>malign</u> the names of celebrities by telling false negative stories about them.

(Cat video) I don't want people to <u>malign</u> my name just because I am sitting in a stroller. I mean, why speak badly about me? I haven't done anything to you.

Definition:_____

_____

10. Massive

The Titanic was a <u>massive</u> ship.

(Cat video) People say I look <u>massive</u> in this picture. I am not this big in real life.

Definition:_____

_____

List 1
Part 6

Very Common ASVAB Vocabulary Words

Memento to Perpetual

1. Memento

Upon visiting the Statue of Liberty, Nellie bought a postcard as a <u>memento</u> of her trip.

(Cat video) I went on a tour of a bicycle factory, and I brought this little bicycle home as a <u>memento</u> of my trip. It is nice to have something to remember my trip by.

Definition:_____

_____

2. Militant

The <u>militant</u> group was very aggressive in their teachings and sought to overthrow the government.

(Cat video) There are many <u>militant</u> groups out there who are aggressive and ready to fight.

Definition:_____

_____

3. Momentous

Graduating from high school is a <u>momentous</u> occasion that people will remember for a long time.

(Cat video) The day my brothers and I were rescued was a <u>momentous</u> occasion. It was a very important day in our lives.

Definition:_____

_____

4. Objective

A judge needs to remain <u>objective</u> in a case, being fair and acknowledging both parties' version of events.

(Cat video) We are lucky that our owner is very <u>objective</u>. She was fair enough to make sure each of us had our own bed.

Definition:_____

_____

5. Obliterated

The bomb <u>obliterated</u> the entire town.

(Cat video) These are the only birds I am allowed to spend time with after I <u>obliterated</u> all the birds in the backyard, but I am a cat. I just can't help killing all the birds I meet.

Definition:_____

_____

6. Obscure

The view of the ocean was <u>obscure</u> because of the fog.

(Cat video) The cloudy sky is causing an <u>obscure</u> moon tonight. I really can't see the moon very well.

Definition:_____

_____

7. Obsolete

Record players are <u>obsolete</u> and have been replaced by more advanced musical technology.

(Cat video) I needed to make a phone call, and they hand me this <u>obsolete</u> phone. I mean, who uses a rotary phone now? Talk about out of date!

Definition:_____

_____

8. Obstinate

The <u>obstinate</u> 3-year-old girl would not give in to what her mother wanted and kept trying to get her way.

(Cat video) I get called <u>obstinate</u> because I don't want to get out of this bag. They call me stubborn. Well, maybe I don't feel like letting the cat out of the bag.

Definition:_____

_____

9. Offish

The unfriendly girl was called <u>offish</u> by her coworkers.

(Cat video) People think Snuggles is <u>offish</u> just because he's not friendly like I am.

Definition:_____

_____

10. Perpetual

The earth travels <u>perpetually</u> around the sun, always has, always will.

(Cat video) Snuggles and I have a <u>perpetual</u> friendship. We will be friends forever.

Definition:_____

_____

List 1
Part 7

Very Common ASVAB Words

Plausible to Timid

1. Plausible

The child offered a <u>plausible</u> explanation as to why the cookies were missing from the cookie jar.

(Cat video) The suspect offered a <u>plausible</u> explanation as to where he was the night of the crime. It was definitely a believable explanation.

Definition:_____

_____

2. Prestige

There is a certain amount of <u>prestige</u> that comes with attending an Ivy League college.

(Cat video) There is a great amount of <u>prestige</u> that comes with being an Internet sensation. I know I have made a lot of great achievements and influences in my life.

Definition:_____

_____

3. Proficient

After learning French for 6 years, Amelia was <u>proficient</u> in the language.

(Cat video) I am <u>proficient</u> at climbing. That is one of the many things that cats are skilled at.

Definition:_____

_____

4. Ravage

The home was <u>ravaged</u> by the fire, and much repair was needed to restore it.

(Cat video) When we arrived at the scene of the crime, we were notified by the fire department that the home had been <u>ravaged</u> by the fire, and it was left in complete destruction.

Definition:_____

_____

5. Relinquished

Martha <u>relinquished</u> her purse to the robber because she knew it was easier to give it up than to fight him.

(Cat video) The woman <u>relinquished</u> her purse to the robber. She knew it was easier to give it up than to try to fight him.

Definition:_____

_____

6. Rudiments/Rudimentary

In basic training, people learn the <u>rudiments</u> of life in the Army.

In elementary school, children gain a <u>rudimentary</u> understanding of reading, writing and arithmetic.

(Cat video) In basic training and boot camp, people learn the <u>rudiments</u> of military life. That is where they learn all the basic principles.

Definition:_____

_____

7. Savory

Thanksgiving dinner with all its special dishes is a <u>savory</u> meal.

(Cat video) Pardon me for talking while I am eating, but I am just enjoying this <u>savory</u> salmon dinner, and boy, is it delicious!

Definition:_____

_____

8. Sturdy

The young weightlifter had a <u>sturdy</u> build.

(Cat video) I like this shirt. It makes me look <u>sturdy</u>. I like to look strong.

Definition:_____

_____

9. Thrift

The widow's <u>thrift</u> is what helped her to raise her large family on such a small income.

(Cat video) I was always taught to use <u>thrift</u> when it comes to spending my money. I make sure I don't spend too much, that way I have enough for myself when I get older.

Definition:_____

_____

10. Timid

The <u>timid</u> girl whispered when she spoke in class.

(Cat video) I have to do all the talking around here. Snuggles is the <u>timid</u> one. He is too shy to talk.

Definition:_____

_____

List 1
Part 8

Very Common ASVAB Words

Turmoil to Zeal

1. Turmoil

The bank was in a state of turmoil when the bank robbery occurred, and all the customers ran out the door screaming.

(Cat video) This might look like turmoil to you, but I can assure you there is no confusion here. I am just spending time with my animal friends.

Definition:_____

_____

2. Unison

The choir sings in unison with all voices united.

(Cat video) Okay, ready guys. We're going to recite this one in unison. On the count of three: one, two, three… The three little kittens they lost their mittens, and they began to cry. Hey, wait a minute. How come I am the only one saying this? I thought we were saying this all together.

Definition:_____

_____

3. Utilize

The mechanic will utilize his jack the next time he changes a flat tire.

(Cat video) I decided to utilize my great personality to help people learn. I know I have to use my gifts in life.

Definition:_____

_____

4. Vague

Emily has a <u>vague</u> memory of her childhood years since she started losing her memory in her old age.

(Cat video) When I asked my friend if I should wear this outfit to the party, he said, "It depends." He gave me such a <u>vague</u> answer. I don't like unclear answers like that.

Definition:_____

_____

5. Wary

I have always been <u>wary</u> of walking through an alley as a shortcut because I know it is not usually a safe place.

(Cat video) I like to tell people make sure you are <u>wary</u> at night. When you go for a walk, always stop and look over your shoulder. Make sure you are cautious. Stay safe out there, people.

Definition:_____

_____

6. *Zeal/Zealous/Zealot

The excited baseball fan cheered for his team with <u>zeal.</u>

The <u>zealous</u> fan cheered for his team with all his strength.

The political activist was considered a <u>zealot</u> because he was very extreme in his beliefs.

(Cat video) My owner is a <u>zealous</u> supporter of animal rights. I am lucky that she is so passionate about caring for animals because if she wasn't, I might never have been rescued.

Definition:_____

_____

Very Common ASVAB Vocabulary Words
Definitions

Part 1
1. Abdicate - to give up or surrender responsibility
2. Abhor - to hate/Abhorrence- feeling of hating something or being disgusted by something
3. Abscond - to leave quickly and secretly
4. Accost - to approach and speak to in a bold way
5. Adept - skilled
6. Ardent - passionate burning
7. Arrogant - full of pride
8. Articulate - speaking clearly
9. Augment - to increase or improve
10. Authentic - genuine, real

Part 2
1. Blatant - outright
2. Blemish - flaw or defect
3. Brevity - briefness
4. Brusque - rudely brief
5. Cease - to stop
6. Chide - to scold or express disapproval of
7. Cumbersome - burdensome, difficult to carry
8. Cursory - on the surface, superficial
9. Detest - to hate
10. Digress - to wander from a subject in talking or writing

Part 3
1. Disdain - to look down upon someone or despise them
2. Domicile - home, residence
3. Economical - not wasting money, thrifty
4. Flaunt - to show off
5. Frail - weak
6. Frugal - not wasteful, being careful with money, thrifty, economical
7. Ghastly - horrible, frightful
8. Grievous - very severe or serious/Grievance- a complaint against something viewed as wrong
9. Hale - healthy
10. Haughty - arrogant

Part 4
1. Hilarious - funny
2. Hostile - aggressive
3. Immaculate - very clean
4. Impair - weaken
5. Imperative - necessary, urgent

6. Impertinent - rude
7. Impetuous - acting with little thought, impulsive
8. Incognito - in disguise
9. Incoherent - unable to be understood
10. Indigent - poor, humble

Part 5
1. Inflexible - not flexible, stiff, rigid
2. Inhabit - to live in
3. Innate - inborn
4. Intermittent - stopping and starting at intervals
5. Judicious - fair
6. Latent - hidden
7. Listless - lifeless
8. Lofty - very high, grand
9. Malign - to speak badly about someone
10. Massive - very large

Part 6
1. Memento - a souvenir, something to help remember a time or place
2. Militant - aggressive, ready to fight
3. Momentous - very important
4. Objective - fair
5. Obliterated - destroyed
6. Obscure - dark or not easily seen
7. Obsolete - no longer in use, out of date
8. Obstinate - stubborn
9. Offish - unfriendly
10. Perpetual - lasting forever

Part 7
1. Plausible - believable
2. Prestige - association with high achievement or influence
3. Proficient - skilled
4. Ravage - to cause destruction or ruin
5. Relinquish - to give up
6. Rudiments/Rudimentary - basic principles
7. Savory - tasty
8. Sturdy - strong
9. Thrift - to be careful with money, economical
10. Timid - shy

Part 8
1. Turmoil - great confusion or uncertainty
2. Unison - action or speech done all at the same time
3. Utilize - to use

4. Vague - unclear
5. Wary - cautious or careful
6. Zeal/Zealous/Zealot - to show enthusiasm or passion

Common ASVAB Vocabulary Review

List 2
Part 1

Common ASVAB Vocabulary Words

Acclaim to Amity

1. Acclaim

The award-winning book received much <u>acclaim</u> from its readers.

(Cat video) As a superhero, I have received much <u>acclaim</u> for all my heroic deeds. There are many people who have given me their approval.

Definition:_____

_____

2. Acute

Marvin had an <u>acute</u> pain in his side, and he rushed to the hospital.

(Cat video) I have an <u>acute</u> pain in my stomach. I haven't had a pain this sharp or this severe. I better head over to the vet before it gets really serious.

Definition:_____

_____

3. Adamant

The politician is <u>adamant</u> about his views on tax reform and is unwilling to change his opinion for anyone.

(Cat video) In the military, your sergeants are very <u>adamant</u> about their demands. They are inflexible, and they are not changing their minds about what they expect you to do.

Definition:_____

_____

4. Adroit

Molly is an <u>adroit</u> skier who won an award for her skiing ability.

(Cat video) I am very <u>adroit</u> at climbing. Climbing is one of the many things that cats are skilled at.

Definition:_____

_____

5. Aesthetic

The art lover was impressed with the appearance of the <u>aesthetic</u> painting.

(Cat video) I hope you appreciate the <u>aesthetics</u> of my appearance. I spend a lot of time trying to show off my beauty.

Definition:_____

_____

6. Agile

The track star is quite <u>agile</u> and was able to jump over hurdles very easily.

(Cat video) Cats are very <u>agile</u>. We move quite easily and quickly.

Definition:_____

_____

7. Ambidextrous

Brett is <u>ambidextrous</u> and sees advantages of being equally skilled with both hands.

(Cat video) I'm <u>ambidextrous,</u> meaning I'm equally skilled at using both hands. So, just because I carry my sword in my right hand doesn't mean I can't equally use it in my left hand.

Definition:_____

_____

8. Ambiguous

The teacher gave <u>ambiguous</u> directions for the assignment, and the class was not sure what to do.

(Cat video) I don't like when people give me <u>ambiguous</u> answers. I asked my friend, "Does this wig look good on me?" He said, "Maybe." I mean his answer was not clear at all. Did he mean yes or did he mean no? I don't like when people are vague like that.

Definition:_____

_____

9. Amenable

Amelia is a cooperative employee and is <u>amenable</u> to suggestions from coworkers on how to improve her work plan.

(Cat video) When you look at me in this crazy outfit, you should realize that I am <u>amenable</u>. I am open to all kinds of suggestions, and I never complain.

Definition:_____

_____

10. Amity

The leaders of many world democracies have a sense of <u>amity</u> and have positive relationships.

(Cat video) There is a great amount of <u>amity</u> between my dog friends and me. We have very peaceful and friendly relations.

Definition:_____

_____

List 2
Part 2

Common ASVAB Vocabulary Words

Apathy to Benevolent

1. Apathy

The criminal lacked <u>apathy</u> for the crimes he committed and did not look sorry in court.

(Cat video) When I step inside the ring with my opponent, I have total <u>apathy</u> for him. You know what that means? That means I feel nothing because my goal is to get in there, knock him out, and hold onto my championship belt.

Definition:_____

_____

2. Appease

The parents of the kidnapped child decided to <u>appease</u> the kidnapper by giving him the money he asked for in exchange for the child.

(Cat video) We needed to <u>appease</u> the criminal who held people hostage. We satisfied his demands so that he would release the people he had captured.

Definition:_____

_____

3. Apt

Mackenzie can play the piano and the trumpet and is <u>apt</u> to pick up a third instrument quite easily.

(Cat video) Cats are <u>apt</u> to climb to high places. What can I say? We are just quick to learn how to do it.

Definition:_____

_____

4. Aquatic

Dolphins are <u>aquatic</u> animals that cannot live on land.

(Cat video) I am spending time with my <u>aquatic</u> friends. It is interesting how so many different types of animals live in the water.

Definition:_____

_____

5. Astute

The <u>astute</u> businessman used his intelligence and common sense to build a successful business.

(Cat video) When people see me wearing my glasses, they tend to call me <u>astute</u>. For some reason, they just assume that I am clever or wise just because I wear glasses.

Definition:_____

_____

6. Austere

In the 1800s, life on the prairie was very <u>austere</u>, and people lacked many of the basic necessities in life.

(Cat video) My brothers and I lived an <u>austere</u> lifestyle before we were rescued. We were living in severe conditions.

Definition:_____

_____

7. Auxiliary

The <u>auxiliary</u> police provide assistance to the police department.

(Cat video) People often question me about being in the police department, but I need to explain to them I am not a regular police officer. I am part of the <u>auxiliary</u> police department. We are the group that helps out the police.

Definition:_____

_____

8. Barred

Cell phones are <u>barred</u> from schools because children would be distracted from learning if they brought them to school.

(Cat video) I am <u>barred</u> from going on the counters, but do you think that just because I am not allowed means I am going to stop doing it? Like, no way!

Definition:_____

_____

9. Belligerent

The <u>belligerent</u> high school student spent much time in detention for fighting with others.

(Cat video) We, pirates, have a reputation for being <u>belligerent</u> because we are always ready to fight. Arrgh!

Definition:_____

_____

10. Benevolent

The man was very <u>benevolent</u> and gave of his time and his money freely to those in need.

(Cat video) I set up a <u>benevolent</u> organization in which I give money to animal right's groups. It is very important for me to practice being kind and charitable.

Definition:_____

_____

List 2
Part 3

Common ASVAB Vocabulary Words

Bland to Corrugated

1. Bland

When Martha found out she had an ulcer, the doctor put her on a <u>bland</u> diet since spicy foods made her ulcer worse.

(Cat video) As a chef, I am aware that some people need to stay on <u>bland</u> diets that are mild and lacking in flavor because of certain health issues.

Definition:_____

_____

2. Boggy

The <u>boggy</u> land near the bay was too moist to plant any vegetables.

(Cat video) I'm dressed up as a cactus. Cacti need to live in dry land. They could never survive in <u>boggy</u> land, which is wet and moist land.

Definition:_____

_____

3. Calligraphy

The bride-to-be had her wedding invitations written in <u>calligraphy</u> since fancy handwriting is often seen on those invitations.

(Cat video) Today I will be giving lessons on how to write in <u>calligraphy</u>. Calligraphy is the fancy handwriting that you can see in many different situations. One of which is wedding invitations.

Definition:_____

_____

4. Carcass

After the deer was hit and killed by a car, its <u>carcass</u> lay on the road for a day before it was cleaned up.

(Cat video) Here I am, dressed up as a lion. How do you think I feel with this costume that just looks like a <u>carcass</u> on me? I mean, really, it's like carrying around a dead body of an animal.

Definition:_____

_____

5. Chronic

Martha was in <u>chronic</u> pain and needed to see a doctor about her nonstop suffering.

(Cat video) I have a cough I just can't seem to get rid of. Excuse me. I better go to the vet before it becomes <u>chronic</u>. The last thing I need is a cough that lasts for a really long time.

Definition:_____

_____

6. Compatible

The two girls were very <u>compatible</u> and became great friends.

(Cat video) Snuggles and I are <u>compatible</u>. We are good friends, and we get along very well.

Definition:_____

_____

7. Competent

Morgan is a <u>competent</u> soldier. As result, she is being promoted very quickly.

(Cat video) Military training is meant to prove who is <u>competent</u> of being part of the military. It shows who is adequate or capable of serving our nation.

Definition:_____

_____

8. Complacent

The child was <u>complacent</u> with the number of presents she received for Christmas and did not expect any more.

(Cat video) I am so <u>complacent</u> in this position. I mean look at the comfort! I am so self-satisfied here.

Definition:_____

_____

9. Consequences

In order to correct poor behavior, children must know there will be <u>consequences</u> for misbehaving.

(Cat video) When you train hard at the gym like I do, you can enjoy the <u>consequences</u>. It is great to have wonderful results from your hard work.

Definition:_____

_____

10. Corrugated

The roof was made with <u>corrugated</u> metal, and its grooves helped the rain to flow freely.

(Cat video) Snuggles, check out this box. It's made out of <u>corrugated</u> cardboard. If you look closely, there are grooves inside the cardboard that make it extra strong. This is probably a good place for our naps.

Definition:_____

_____

List 2
Part 4

Common ASVAB Vocabulary Words

Credible to Deplore

1. Credible

The police found a credible witness to the crime, and they knew his testimony was believable.

(Cat video) We found a credible witness at the scene of the crime. This witness told a believable story, and now we are on the search for the suspect.

Definition:_____

_____

2. Credulous

The young child was credulous since he believed anything he heard.

(Cat video) My problem is I am too credulous. I believe anything anyone tells me. When they said to me, "Come on. Dress up in pajamas and sit in a high chair. It will be fun." I believed them, and look at me now!

Definition:_____

_____

3. Curt

When Troy's mother asked how his day was, he gave her a curt response, "Don't ask." His rudeness made her realize he had a tough day.

(Cat video) When I am working at the pet store as a security guard, sometimes I need to be curt. I need to be rudely brief with customers whose behavior is not acceptable.

Definition:_____

_____

4. Curtail

In order to lose weight, Margie decided to curtail her eating of sweets.

(Cat video) Hello Mr. Rat, I am sorry to inform you that your life is about to be curtailed. I am a cat. You are a rat. Your life is about to be cut short very soon.

Definition:_____

_____

5. Debonair

The older gentleman looked very debonair with his neatly parted hair while wearing his three-piece suit, new leather shoes, and a pocket watch.

(Cat video) Don't I look so debonair in my bowtie? I mean, I'm confident, I'm stylish, and I'm charming.

Definition:_____

_____

6. Deft

Rachel was a deft musician and earned many medals for her ability to play.

(Cat video) I am very deft at climbing. Being this skilled lets me get on top of the cabinets whenever I want.

Definition:_____

_____

7. Defunct

Since Alvin's computer was now defunct and could not be fixed, he decided to buy a new one.

(Cat video) I tried to start my car today, and I realized it was defunct, sitting here dead. I called the repair shop. They are sending out a tow truck to bring it right in, and they said, "No problem. We will have it up and running in no time."

Definition:_____

_____

8. Defy

The bratty teenager will <u>defy</u> his mother's rules.

(Cat video) Sometimes I <u>defy</u> my owner. When she tells me to get off the counter, I say, "Nope!" and I don't do what she tells me to do.

Definition:_____

_____

9. Deplete

Using too much paper will cause people will cut down more trees and <u>deplete</u> the forests.

(Cat video) When I work out, I train so hard I <u>deplete</u> all my energy. So when I get home, I make sure I have a good healthy meal to replace all the energy I used up.

Definition:_____

_____

10. Deplore

The animal rights activists <u>deplore</u> the actions of those who wear fur coats.

(Cat video) I <u>deplore</u> the mistreatment of animals. This is something of which I disapprove.

Definition:_____

_____

List 2
Part 5

Common ASVAB Vocabulary Words

Destitute to Divert

1. Destitute/Destitution

After losing his job and using up his savings, Roy was <u>destitute</u>.

Living as an unemployed actor led Hal into a life of <u>destitution</u>.

(Cat video) Before we were adopted, we were <u>destitute</u>. We lived in extreme poverty, and we had nothing at all to eat.

Definition:

2. Diffident

The <u>diffident</u> young girl was too shy to speak in front of her class.

(Cat video) Everyone knows that Snuggles is the <u>diffident</u> one. I am outgoing. He is shy. What can I say? We are just different cats.

Definition:

3. Disburse

The company will <u>disburse</u> paychecks to its employees every Thursday.

(Cat video) I am going to <u>disburse</u> the salaries of my employees because today is payday.

Definition:

4. Discern

On the math test, the students needed to <u>discern</u> the pattern of numbers to determine what number should come next.

(Cat video) Can you <u>discern</u> the pattern that is behind me on the board? Is it possible to figure out or to make out a pattern and decide what comes next? Let's see. 1, 3, 5, 7… Hmm… They are all odd numbers. We are skipping the evens so it looks like the next number would be 9.

Definition:_____

_____

5. Dismay

Much to Mary Ellen's <u>dismay,</u> she found out she had a tumor.

(Cat video) When I found out I had to wear this wig, it was much to my <u>dismay</u>. Talk about disappointment!

Definition:_____

_____

6. Dispel

The reporter interviewed the celebrity to <u>dispel</u> the false stories that were being told about him once and for all.

(Cat video) I am going to <u>dispel</u> a myth about cats. People say you cannot train cats. Let me break up this falsehood and get rid of it because I have three words for you, "Look at me!"

Definition:_____

_____

7. Disperse

The farmer will <u>disperse</u> seeds to plant in the fields.

(Cat video) As bees, we <u>disperse</u> pollen. By doing this, we spread pollen all over, and we help plants to grow.

Definition:_____

_____

8. Disrupt

The barking dog next door will <u>disrupt</u> my sleep.

(Cat video) When I work my security job at the pet store, sometimes loud dogs come in and <u>disrupt</u> the peace. They disturb and interrupt the quietness of our store.

Definition:_____

_____

9. Diverge

Lisa gave directions to Stacy and told her to make a left when the two roads would <u>diverge.</u>

(Cat video) When Snuggles and I are taken for walks, we <u>diverge</u> in two different directions. He is driven south, and I am driven north.

Definition:_____

_____

10. Divert

Jacob loses focus easily since any distraction can <u>divert</u> his attention.

(Cat video) Can you see the way I'm dressed up? That's what happens when people <u>divert</u> your attention. They just distract you with things like treats, and next thing you know you're wearing a bathrobe, a ribbon around your head, and holding onto a toy mouse.

Definition:_____

_____

List 2
Part 6

Common ASVAB Vocabulary Words

Divulge to Feud

1. Divulge

Reina decided to <u>divulge</u> her secrets to her best friend since she was the only one she trusted.

(Cat video) I am going to <u>divulge</u> a little secret. When no one is looking, I jump up on the table, and I steal one piece of meat out of everyone's plate. Boy, it feels good to finally reveal that.

Definition:_____

_____

2. Eccentric

The <u>eccentric</u> woman talked to herself in the grocery store.

(Cat video) Sometimes people think I am an <u>eccentric</u> cat just because I wear a wig, beads, sunglasses, and clothes, but I'm really not an odd or unusual cat at all.

Definition:_____

_____

3. Edible

Olivia loves her <u>edible</u> treat since it tastes so good.

(Cat video) I hope you realize I am not <u>edible</u>. You cannot eat me. I am not a hot dog. I am a hot Internet sensation who happens to be a cat.

Definition:_____

_____

4. Efface

The eraser will <u>efface</u> all that Suzanne has written on the paper.

(Cat video) Can someone hand me the eraser? I need to <u>efface</u> the writing on the board.

Definition:_____

_____

5. Eject

Harry will <u>eject</u> his CD from the player when the song is over.

(Cat video) When I work my security job at the pet store, sometimes I have to <u>eject</u> certain pets. Their behavior is not appropriate, and they need to be removed.

Definition:_____

_____

6. Elated

The child will be <u>elated</u> when she will receive the present she always wanted.

(Cat video) When I found out I was going for a stroller ride, I was <u>elated</u>. Boy, going for rides really makes me happy.

Definition:_____

_____

7. Eulogy

The pastor gave a <u>eulogy</u> at the man's funeral making sure to tell about all his good qualities.

(Cat video) We are gathered here today for me to give a <u>eulogy</u> about Fluffy. Fluffy was a good cat. He only once ate a bird. He never ate anyone else's food, and he never ever went outside the litter box. Let us bow our heads and remember Fluffy.

Definition:_____

_____

8. Famished

The children were <u>famished</u> because they had not eaten all day.

(Cat video) I'm so hungry. I'm <u>famished</u>. So, pardon me while I steal a chicken cutlet.

Definition:_____

_____

9. Feigned

Isabella <u>feigned</u> interest in sports just to fit in with the boys who loved sports.

(Cat video) This rat <u>feigned</u> death. He hoped that by faking his death he would get a chance to run away from me, but it's not going to work.

Definition:_____

_____

10. Feud

There is a long time <u>feud</u> going on between the two families, and no one remembers how all the fighting started.

(Cat video) When you live as a pirate, you're always ready for a <u>feud</u> because fighting is just part of your lifestyle.

Definition:_____

_____

List 2
Part 7

Common ASVAB Vocabulary Words

Fidget to Grim

1. Fidget

The 5-year-old boy could not sit still and began to <u>fidget</u>.

(Cat video) This rat is starting to <u>fidget</u>. I can see he is getting restless and making nervous movements because he knows what is about to happen to him.

Definition:_____

_____

2. Fluorescent

The <u>fluorescent</u> light attracted many moths with its brightness.

(Cat video) I love the <u>fluorescent</u> lights from my glow stick around my neck. That way when I am in the dark, you can see my bright lights shining.

Definition:_____

_____

3. Forlorn

The dog at the shelter looked so <u>forlorn</u> and was staring at us with the saddest eyes hoping for attention.

(Cat video) I am very <u>forlorn</u> today. Today is the anniversary of Fluffy's death, and I feel so very sad.

Definition:_____

_____

4. Futile

No matter how hard Julian searched to find a job, his attempts were <u>futile</u>; he remained unemployed.

(Cat video) Many people think that toilet training a cat is <u>futile</u>. But I say, it isn't useless at all if your cat is smart like me.

Definition:_____

_____

5. Genesis

When Alexander Graham Bell invented the telephone, it was the <u>genesis</u> of the use of telephones in our world.

(Cat video) This picture is from the <u>genesis</u> of my life as a rescue. This is the very beginning, when I was found, just my brothers and me.

Definition:_____

_____

6. Germane

When Stephanie went for a job interview, her employee asked her <u>germane</u> questions about her job history. The questions were relevant to her suitability to the job at hand.

(Cat video) One student in my class did not focus well, and I reminded him to focus on topics that were <u>germane</u> to the class subject.

Definition:_____

_____

7. Glut

At Thanksgiving dinner, there was a <u>glut</u> of food, too much for the family to eat.

(Cat video) If you stop by the North Pole on Christmas Eve, you will see there is a <u>glut</u> of toys. It seems like there are too many of them, but you will realize we are giving toys to every child around the world.

Definition:_____

_____

8. Grating

The loud buzzing of the microphone was a <u>grating</u> sound that made the audience cover their ears.

(Cat video) If there is one thing that really gets on my nerves, it's the <u>grating</u> sound of nails scratching across the chalkboard. That has to be the most irritating sound out there!

Definition:_____

_____

9. Gratis

The basket of bread was <u>gratis</u> with the meal and did not cost anything extra.

(Cat video) All the toys that Santa gives to children are <u>gratis</u>. That's right. They are free.

Definition:_____

_____

10. Grim

The doctors gave the Caleb a <u>grim</u> diagnosis, and he knew he did not have much time left to live.

(Cat video) Shortly before Fluffy died, we received the <u>grim</u> news from the vet that he wasn't going to get any better. We had to deal with this sad fact.

Definition:_____

_____

List
Part 8

Common ASVAB Vocabulary Words

Gross to Homogenous

1. Gross

The moldy bread had a <u>gross</u> appearance.

(Cat video) This ugly wig makes me have a <u>gross</u> appearance.

Definition:_____

_____

2. Grotesque

Some crime shows present very <u>grotesque</u> scenes of bodies that are quite disturbing.

(Cat video) I look so <u>grotesque</u> with this wig on. I mean, talk about a distorted appearance. Ugh!

Definition:_____

_____

3. Gruesome

The haunted house presented many <u>gruesome</u> scenes to scare its patrons.

(Cat video) On Halloween, we like to decorate with many <u>gruesome</u> decorations so people are filled with horror when they see ghosts and goblins and witches.

Definition:_____

_____

4. Gullible

The trusting wife was very <u>gullible</u> and believed all of her husband's lies.

(Cat video) My brothers and I were pretty <u>gullible</u> when we got rescued. We were so easily fooled. All we hear is "Here kitty, kitty." Next thing we know, we are living in someone's house. But you know what, we came out pretty good.

Definition:_____

_____

5. Guttural

Many sounds in Hebrew are <u>guttural</u> and are produced in the throat.

(Cat video) When I gargle, I make a <u>guttural</u> sound. It comes from deep in the back of my throat. Listen up. (gargling sounds)

Definition:_____

_____

6. Haphazard

Bethany's method of cleaning her house was not organized, but was <u>haphazard</u> and random.

(Cat video) People ask me for advice on how to win the lottery, but I tell them the numbers are selected in a <u>haphazard</u> way. There is no pattern; it's just completely random.

Definition:_____

_____

7. Hardy

The <u>hardy</u> plants were strong enough to survive the winter.

(Cat video) When I applied for the security job, I was told they needed a <u>hardy</u> employee. That's right. Someone who is strong and bold like me.

Definition:_____

_____

8. Hoax

The notification about the actor's death was a <u>hoax</u> since he was alive and well.

(Cat video) We're cracking down on people that are running the <u>hoax</u> of shell games on the side of the street. They give you three cups. They hide something under a cup. They say you bet on it, and you guess which cup. Well, guess what? It is a <u>hoax</u>. There is nothing under any of the cups. You will lose your money. So, be cautious.

Definition:_____

_____

9. Hoist

The custodian will <u>hoist</u> the flag up the flagpole in the morning.

(Cat video) On Christmas Eve, all the elves help Santa to <u>hoist</u> all the bags of toys onto his sled. It isn't easy, but we help him to lift them all up.

Definition:_____

_____

10. Homogenous

The <u>homogenous</u> group of students was all functioning at the same level in reading and math.

(Cat video) The two of us are a <u>homogenous</u> pair. We have a lot of similarities.

Definition:_____

_____

List 2
Part 9

Common ASVAB Vocabulary Words

Horrendous to Inclement

1. Horrendous

After committing a <u>horrendous</u> crime, the woman was sentenced to life in prison.

(Cat video) When my owner first told me to use the litter box, I said, "This is <u>horrendous</u>." What a horrible set up! What does she think I am, some kind of animal or something?

Definition:_____

_____

2. Humid

The tropical rain forest has a <u>humid</u> climate, and is often very damp and muggy.

(Cat video) Today is such a <u>humid</u> day. It is so damp and wet out there. I made sure I put on my rain gear.

Definition:_____

_____

3. Humorous

The child told a <u>humorous</u> joke and made everyone laugh.

How are pumpkins like cats? Because they are both waiting on the porch for you when you get home. Am I <u>humorous</u> or what? I hope you think I am funny.

Definition:_____

_____

4. Illicit

Many drugs are <u>illicit</u> in our country, and many people are arrested for possessing them.

(Cat video) As a security guard in the pet store, I need to make sure there are no <u>illicit</u> activities going on in the business. I am looking out for illegal activities like dogs eating biscuits before they pay for them.

Definition:_____

_____

5. Illusion

The fun house mirrors gave the <u>illusion</u> that Timothy had no neck.

(Cat video) Don't live under the <u>illusion</u> that basic training or boot camp will be easy. Don't live holding that false idea in your head because it's going to be rough. I guarantee it!

Definition:_____

_____

6. Impromptu

Without any preparation, the best man stood up and gave an <u>impromptu</u> speech at the wedding.

(Cat video) I saw a freshly folded pile of laundry, and I decided to have a little <u>impromptu</u> nap here. I didn't plan for this nap. It wasn't prepared, but I was just so comfortable. Aaah…

Definition:_____

_____

7. Impudent

The <u>impudent</u> man on the subway pushed Pearl out of the way so he could catch his train.

(Cat video) Many people refer to me as <u>impudent</u> because I have such confidence when I walk into a room. They know I am bold and fearless.

Definition:_____

_____

8. Incendiary

The <u>incendiary</u> device had the ability to start a fire.

(Cat video) Fireworks are <u>incendiary</u> devices. People need to be very cautious. As a firefighter, I see a lot of accidents because these fireworks can explode or cause fire.

Definition: _____

_____

9. Incinerate

If the firemen cannot put out the fire, it will <u>incinerate</u> all the buildings on the block.

(Cat video) By the time the fire department arrived at the scene, the entire house had been <u>incinerated</u>. It was completely destroyed by the fire.

Definition:_____

_____

10. Inclement

The students will play inside when there is <u>inclement</u> weather and will play outside only when the weather is nice.

(Cat video) I am prepared for the <u>inclement</u> weather. I took out my rain gear so I am dressed appropriately for the rough and stormy weather that is coming today.

Definition:_____

_____

List 2
Part 10

Common ASVAB Vocabulary Words

Indelible to Ingenuous

1. Indelible

The indelible ink spilled on Josephine's shirt, and the stain would not come out in the laundry.

(Cat video) Looks like someone scribbled all over this board with indelible ink. I don't know what we are going to do now because this is permanent. It can't be erased.

Definition:_____

_____

2. Indifferent

Many voters have a favorite political candidate in the election while others remain indifferent.

(Cat video) When it comes to politics, I like to remain indifferent. It is easy to remain neutral when you are a cat.

Definition:_____

_____

3. Indispensable

The bookkeeper was an indispensable part of the company since the business would not run properly without her.

(Cat video) Armor is an indispensable item for a warrior. It is absolutely necessary in battle.

Definition:_____

_____

4. Inept

Rosemarie was fired because her boss considered her to be an <u>inept</u> employee.

(Cat video) When I train people, I don't want anyone who is <u>inept</u>. So if you're unfit or you're unskilled, don't waste my time.

Definition: _____

_____

5. Inertia

Isaac Newton taught people about <u>inertia</u>, the fact that objects at rest remain at rest, while objects in motion remain in motion.

When I need to explain Newton's Laws of Motion, I think about <u>inertia</u>. An object at rest remains at rest while an object in motion remains in motion. Just like me with my workouts, if I stay on the couch I am going to stay there, but once I get working out, there is no stopping me.

Definition: _____

_____

6. Infallible

No one in the world is <u>infallible</u> since everyone makes mistakes sometimes.

(Cat video) Children often think that Santa is <u>infallible</u>. They think he can't make any mistakes, but I'm telling you, no one's perfect.

Definition: _____

_____

7. Infinite

Many people believe the universe is <u>infinite</u>, while others believe it does not extend without limits.

(Cat video) When you read, your ability to learn is <u>infinite</u>. There is no limit to what you can learn from reading.

Definition: _____

_____

8. Infinitesimal

The microscope helped the scientist to see the <u>infinitesimal</u> virus that was too small to be seen with the naked eye.

(Cat video) When I want to get a better look at <u>infinitesimal</u> objects, I use my microscope. It's the only way that you can really look at some things that are very small.

Definition:_____

_____

9. Ingenious

The scientist's <u>ingenious</u> experiments led him to amazing discoveries that were admired by many.

(Cat video) Toilet training your cat is an <u>ingenious</u> idea. I mean, think of how clever it is.

Definition:_____

_____

10. Ingenuous

The young child was <u>ingenuous</u> and opened the door to the robber since she was too trusting.

(Cat video) This picture captures my <u>ingenuous</u> nature. I am very childlike and innocent, very trusting and open. That's me.

Definition:_____

_____

List 2
Part 11

Common ASVAB Vocabulary Words

Inherent to Laudable

1. Inherent

As a child, Rolando showed an <u>inherent</u> talent at playing the piano even before he ever took lessons.

(Cat video) Being a good napper is an <u>inherent</u> part of being a cat. I didn't have to practice. This ability just exists naturally in me.

Definition:_____

_____

2. Insipid

The professor's lectures were <u>insipid</u>, and many of his students would fall asleep in class.

(Cat video) I was reading a book that was so <u>insipid</u>. It just bored me to sleep.

Definition:_____

_____

3. Instill

Most parents work to <u>instill</u> good values into their children believing that what they teach them will affect their life decisions.

(Cat video) When you are born into a royal family, your family will work to <u>instill</u> proper manners into you. It is something that is at the top of their list of what needs to be put into your mind and actions. By the way, sorry for this costume, but when you are running a one-man show, sometimes you get stuck being a princess.

Definition:_____

_____

4. Integrity

Alice was chosen for the high position at the bank because she was believed to be an honest woman of <u>integrity</u>.

(Cat video) I run my catering business with <u>integrity</u>. My clients know that I am trustworthy and honest.

Definition:_____

_____

5. Jargon

Many professional fields have their own <u>jargon</u> or vocabulary that others would not understand.

(Cat video) As a professor, I use a certain <u>jargon</u> when I speak. That is a specialized vocabulary for people in my profession.

Definition:_____

_____

6. Jeopardy

Anthony is in <u>jeopardy</u> of being expelled after he hacked into the school's records.

(Cat video) When you meet a pirate, your life is in <u>jeopardy</u> because of the danger we put you in when we tell you to walk the plank.

Definition:_____

_____

7. Jetty

Brad docked his boat at the <u>jetty</u>, which was designed to protect the harbor.

(Cat video) When we are out on the pirate ship and we want to dock, we pull up to the <u>jetty</u>, and we dock our boat. Right there is where we find the wall that protects the harbor.

Definition:_____

_____

8. Jubilant

Sabrina was <u>jubilant</u> when she found out she was going to be a big sister and decided to have a party to celebrate.

(Cat video) Being an elf is a great job because I know there are many <u>jubilant</u> children around the world because of my work. Nothing makes me happier than making children joyful.

Definition:_____

_____

9. Knead

The baker will <u>knead</u> the dough to prepare it to be made into a loaf of bread.

(Cat video) When I bake bread, I make sure to <u>knead</u> the dough. I work to press it all together with my hands so it is ready to be baked.

Definition:_____

_____

10. Laudable

Alicia's achievements were <u>laudable</u>, and she received much praise from her family and friends.

(Cat video) Being toilet trained is quite a <u>laudable</u> achievement of mine. I mean I know it is definitely worthy of praise.

Definition:_____

_____

List 2
Part 12

Common ASVAB Vocabulary Words

Lethal to Mammoth

1. Lethal

The death row inmate's life will be ended by a <u>lethal</u> injection.

(Cat video) When you meet a band of pirates while traveling the seven seas, you realize just how <u>lethal</u> we can be. We are a deadly bunch!

Definition:_____

_____

2. Levelheaded

Sydney is very <u>levelheaded</u> and thinks very clearly when she makes big decisions.

(Cat video) Santa always considered me the <u>levelheaded</u> reindeer. He knew I was sensible enough to guide the sled.

Definition:_____

_____

3. Levity

Comedies are filled with <u>levity</u> unlike many dramas that are so serious.

(Cat video) There is a certain amount of <u>levity</u> that comes with dressing up as Santa. It is such a lighthearted costume to wear. I enjoy it.

Definition:_____

_____

4. Limber

Many people called the flexible gymnast <u>limber</u>.

(Cat video) I like to train by jumping rope so I can keep my body <u>limber</u>. It is always good to be flexible in the ring.

Definition:_____

_____

5. Luminous

The lantern was <u>luminous</u> in the dark forest showing Chelsea the way back to the cabin.

(Cat video) I have a <u>luminous</u> band around my neck so when the lights go out and it's time for a dance party, I can glow and have a great time.

Definition:_____

_____

6. Majestic

The <u>majestic</u> palace consisted of such elegance and beauty.

(Cat video) I love the <u>majestic</u> robe I received when I became king. It is so grand and fancy.

Definition:_____

_____

7. Malady

The doctor worked to find a cure for Linda's <u>malady</u>.

(Cat video) I have decided to take it easy until my <u>malady</u> passes. The vet told me to rest until my illness went away.

Definition:_____

_____

8. Malicious

The <u>malicious</u> woman planned to break up her coworker's marriage.

(Cat video) As pirates, we have been known as being <u>malicious</u> because of all the evil and wrongdoing we have done.

Definition:_____

_____

9. Malignant

The brain tumor was <u>malignant</u> which was disappointing news since a cancerous tumor is more difficult to treat.

(Cat video) After I operated on Fluffy, I was able to break the bad news to his family that his tumor was indeed <u>malignant</u>. They were very sad when they heard that he had cancer.

Definition:_____

_____

10. Mammoth

The blue whale is a <u>mammoth</u> animal and is the largest animal on earth.

(Cat video) If I keep bench pressing and deadlifting like this, very soon I am going to be <u>mammoth</u>. Oh yeah, watch out I'll be very large.

Definition:_____

_____

List 2
Part 13

Common ASVAB Vocabulary Words

Manual to Opportune

1. Manual

Lee's job involved <u>manual</u> labor since he skilled in working with his hands.

(Cat video) The toys in Santa's workshop are created by the <u>manual</u> labor of the elves. We create all those toys by hand.

Definition:_____

_____

2. Meager

The widow has a <u>meager</u> amount of food left to eat until her next check arrives.

(Cat video) Before we were rescued, we had a <u>meager</u> amount of food. It really was a small, inadequate amount, and we were very hungry.

Definition:_____

_____

3. Meander

The young boy liked to <u>meander</u> instead of walking on the straight path.

(Cat video) Part of my job as a bee is to <u>meander</u> through the fields and gather up pollen. It isn't easy to wander around all day like I do, but I earn my reputation of being busy as a bee.

Definition:_____

_____

4. Mercenary

The <u>mercenary</u> will do anything for money.

(Cat video) When you work as a <u>mercenary,</u> all you care about is money. Doing the right thing doesn't really matter. You just work for the money.

Definition:_____

_____

5. Meticulous

Vanessa was very exact, and her work was always <u>meticulous</u>.

(Cat video) When it comes to writing research papers, I make sure I am <u>meticulous</u>. I am very exact about the details in my work.

Definition:_____

_____

6. Negligence/Negligent

The parents' <u>negligence</u> of their children was considered to be abusive since they did not care for their basic needs.

The dog's fur was all matted because the care he received from his owner was <u>negligent</u>.

(Cat video) Our mother was very <u>negligent</u> of us. She really left us with nothing to eat. She was very careless, and she failed to do the right thing for her three sons.

Definition:_____

_____

7. Notary

The <u>notary</u> signed and stamped the letter as proof to the insurance company that Mr. Brown was the person he claimed to be.

(Cat video) I recently became a <u>notary</u>. When people need to sign important paperwork, I check their identification and put my stamp on the paper to prove that they are who they say they are.

Definition:_____

_____

8. Notorious

The <u>notorious</u> bank robber was well known for his life of crime.

(Cat video) Pirates like me are <u>notorious</u>. We're famous for the bad things that we do.

Definition:_____

_____

9. Nullify/Null

The politicians in New York State decided to <u>nullify</u> the death penalty so that no one in the state is executed anymore.

When Jessica decided she did not want to buy a fence anymore, the fence company agreed that her contract would be <u>null</u>.

(Cat video) As king, I have the power to <u>nullify</u> laws that I do not think are fair. So under my rule, those laws are no longer in effect.

Definition:_____

_____

10. Opportune

Lexi was presented with a job offer at an <u>opportune</u> time, and she was able to accept it.

(Cat video) This was such an <u>opportune</u> situation for me. Here I am exhausted, and what do I find? A beautiful pile of laundry to take a nap in. Talk about good timing!

Definition:_____

_____

List 2
Part 14

Common ASVAB Vocabulary Words

Opulent to Prodigious

1. Opulent

The wealthy man led an opulent lifestyle and was willing to spend $1,000 on fuel for his boat trip to buy ice cream.

(Cat video) I live an opulent lifestyle. Due to my success, I have become very wealthy.

Definition:_____

_____

2. Panoramic

The scenic site had a panoramic view where we could see the entire canyon.

(Cat video) When I am guiding Santa's sled, I have a panoramic worldview. I have a wide view in all directions.

Definition:_____

_____

3. Pensive

After the death of her loved one, Mildred remained in a pensive mood for many years, often remembering their times together.

(Cat video) I am in a pensive mood today, thinking and reflecting upon the many events of my life.

Definition:_____

_____

4. Petty

When the teen stole $5 from the lady's wallet, it was considered a petty crime since the amount taken was so little.

(Cat video) I don't have any time for people who act petty. I mean I am here to talk about important things. I don't have time to talk about nonsense or anything unimportant so these petty people just need to stay away from me.

Definition:_____

_____

5. Picayune

Deciding what shirt to wear was a picayune issue for Mateo since he had big decisions before him like deciding what career path to take.

(Cat video) The small amount of money that lies before me might seem picayune to you, but I don't see it as worthless or unimportant at all. This is enough to get me a few days of cat food.

Definition:_____

_____

6. Posthumous

The soldier was given the posthumous award of a purple heart, which honored him after his death.

(Cat video) We are giving Fluffy a posthumous award. This award is given for his acts of kindness during his life, but we will be giving it to him after his death.

Definition:_____

_____

7. Potent

The poison was potent and killed the rats.

(Cat video) When I am in beast mode, I assure you I am a potent force. That's right, I am powerful.

Definition:_____

_____

8. Potential

Sarah has the <u>potential</u> to earn a scholarship because of her outstanding grades in school.

(Cat video) When it comes to weightlifting, I have a lot of <u>potential</u>. I have a great amount of ability when it comes to lifting heavy things.

Definition:_____

_____

9. Precocious

The <u>precocious</u> two-year-old was able to read the newspaper.

(Cat video) I have always been very <u>precocious</u>, just so mature at such an early age.

Definition:_____

_____

10. Prodigious

The 600-pound woman had a <u>prodigious</u> appetite, which caused her enormous weight gain.

(Cat video) As elves, we have the <u>prodigious</u> task of creating toys for children around the world. This is an enormous and extensive task, but we are proud of what we do.

Definition:_____

_____

List 2
Part 15

Common ASVAB Vocabulary Words

Profane to Rodent

1. Profane

Profane language was not allowed in school since cursing was against the rules.

Pirates are known for profane language. They often swear and use bad language.

Definition:_____

_____

2. Profess

The criminal will profess that he is innocent because he does not want to go to jail.

(Cat video) I profess to be a supporter of animal rights. This is something I claim to believe in.

Definition:_____

_____

3. Prosperous

Wyatt ran a prosperous business, and he could see that his hard work paid off.

(Cat video) I have been very successful in my career, and I now call myself prosperous due to my wealth.

Definition:_____

_____

4. Quandary

Scarlett is in a quandary since she had two marriage proposals and does not know which one to accept.

(Cat video) I was in a quandary trying to decide what I should wear for Halloween, but then I found this hat, and I was uncertain no more. I knew this was the costume for me.

Definition:_____

_____

5. Quell

Arianna tried to quell Jacob's anger by apologizing for lying to him.

(Cat video) Part of my role in working security is to quell any disruptions that pop up. So, if I see a fight that is about to break out, I make sure I step in and quiet things down.

Definition:_____

_____

6. Rampant

During the winter, the flu is running rampant with thousands of people infected.

(Cat video) There are certain parts of town where crime is rampant and we have to increase our patrol of those areas. We are trying to stop this widespread crime while we still can.

Definition:_____

_____

7. Rescind

When the boss was unhappy with Sebastian's work performance, he wanted to rescind the raise he had given him.

(Cat video) I am cooking for a party for 12 people, and I just ordered a turkey. Now I find out they are all vegetarians, so I am going to have to rescind that order. Let me get on the phone and cancel that immediately.

Definition:_____

_____

8. Retaliate/Retaliation

The owner of the store plans to <u>retaliate</u> against the man who robbed his store, and he feels revenge was acceptable.

The military responded with <u>retaliation</u> against the enemy after the army base had been bombed.

(Cat video) It is never a good idea to start a fight with a pirate because we will <u>retaliate</u> and seek revenge. You will be sorry!

Definition:_____

_____

9. Reticent

The two sisters were very different while one was outgoing and friendly, the other was shy and <u>reticent</u>.

(Cat video) My friend, Snuggles, is often very <u>reticent</u>. He is very quiet and unwilling to speak most of the time.

Definition:_____

_____

10. Rodent

<u>Rodents</u> include mice, rats, and hamsters, among other animals.

(Cat video) How do you like my <u>rodent</u>? He is going to be my snack. This one is a rat. He is one of many mammals whose teeth never stop growing just like mice.

Definition:_____

_____

List 2
Part 16

Common ASVAB Vocabulary Words

Satchel to Spiritual

1. Satchel

Paul carried his books in a <u>satchel</u> that he placed over his shoulder.

(Cat video) I have a new <u>satchel</u>. I am very happy with this bag. It helps me organize my belongings.

Definition:_____

_____

2. Scrappy

The young boxer was <u>scrappy</u> and often started fights with people he met in public.

(Cat video) Pirates are known for being <u>scrappy</u> because we are always ready for a fight.

Definition:_____

_____

3. Shrine

The church had a <u>shrine</u> with a statue for people to visit when praying.

(Cat video) We set up a <u>shrine</u> at Fluffy's grave. We put a few religious items so we could honor him.

Definition:_____

_____

4. Slander

The gossip magazine tends to <u>slander</u> the names of many celebrities when falsely accusing them of crimes.

(Cat video) When you watch boxing press conferences, some people try to <u>slander</u> other people. They speak falsely about them, trying to ruin their reputation, but I don't play like that. I fight fair.

Definition:_____

_____

5. Slender

The models are required to be <u>slender</u> and need to watch their weight.

(Cat video) I am a <u>slender</u> cat. I make sure I eat right and exercise. That's how I stay so slim.

Definition:_____

_____

6. Slovenly

Since the homeless man had no access to a shower, he had a <u>slovenly</u> appearance.

(Cat video) This wig looks so <u>slovenly</u> on me. I mean it is so sloppy, so untidy. I just look like a mess.

Definition:_____

_____

7. Solemn

The funeral was a very <u>solemn</u> event to attend.

(Cat video) The day we lost Fluffy was a very <u>solemn</u> day in our lives. It was very serious.

Definition:_____

_____

8. Sophisticated

Brenda enjoyed going to the opera and felt she was more <u>sophisticated</u> than her friend who enjoyed comedy clubs.

(Cat video) I am known for being very <u>sophisticated</u> because I am knowledgeable about the world.

Definition:_____

_____

9. Sordid

Even though Steve seemed like a good man, he had a <u>sordid</u> past.

(Cat video) As pirates, we are known for our <u>sordid</u> lifestyles. Our histories are often dirty and wretched.

Definition:_____

_____

10. Spiritual

A <u>spiritual</u> person often relies on their faith when life becomes difficult.

(Cat video) I like to get in touch with my <u>spiritual</u> side. I make time to meditate and pray because religion and the soul are very important to me.

Definition:_____

_____

List 2
Part 17
Common ASVAB Vocabulary Words

Sporadic to Terse

1. Sporadic

Ever since Lucille's husband died, she spent much of her time depressed with only <u>sporadic</u> moments of happiness.

(Cat video) I am wearing my rain gear today because the weather forecast predicted <u>sporadic</u> rainstorms. I know they are going to happen randomly, and I don't know exactly where, but I am prepared.

Definition:_____

_____

2. Stalwart

As a <u>stalwart</u> supporter of children's rights, the politician remained dedicated to the hard work involved in stopping child abuse in his community.

(Cat video) All the exercise I do has made me <u>stalwart</u>. I know I am strong, and I am sturdy.

Definition:_____

_____

3. Steadfast

The minister was <u>steadfast</u> in his religious beliefs and would not change them for anyone.

(Cat video) As a boxer, I need to remain <u>steadfast</u>. I am always firm, fixed, and constant in working toward my goals.

Definition:_____

_____

4. Surmount

With motivation and effort, Gabriel realized he could <u>surmount</u> any challenge.

(Cat video) Winning the championship belt was a challenge that I needed to <u>surmount,</u> and I am proud to say that I overcame that challenge.

Definition:_____

_____

5. Tactful/Tact

The doctor was very <u>tactful</u> in delivering the bad news to the patient, making sure he remained positive while being truthful.

The doctor delivered the bad news with <u>tact</u>, trying not to upset his patient.

(Cat video) Santa really needs to be <u>tactful</u> when he lets the other reindeer know that I'm going to be guiding the sled. He has to be able to say the right thing without offending any of them.

Definition:_____

_____

6. Tangible

The Kindergarten teacher collected little prizes for her students since they needed <u>tangible</u> rewards in addition to praise.

(Cat video) I like to decorate for the holidays because when I have a <u>tangible</u> item that I can touch it makes the holidays so much more real to me.

Definition:_____

_____

7. Taut

The <u>taut</u> rubber band eventually broke since it was pulled too tight.

(Cat video) I got these leg warmers for an aerobics class I am teaching, but they are so <u>taut</u> on me. They are so tightly stretched. I don't even think I am going to be able to do half the moves.

Definition:_____

_____

8. Tenacious/Tenacity

The Olympic medalist made it so far because she was <u>tenacious</u> and never gave up.

Because she worked so hard and never gave up, Maya's <u>tenacity</u> allowed her to make it to the Olympics.

(Cat video) To be a successful boxer, you have to be <u>tenacious</u>. Be persistent, and never ever give up!

Definition:_____

_____

9. Tentative

Meredith set up a <u>tentative</u> date for her wedding, but she will have a finalized date soon.

(Cat video) Santa gave me a <u>tentative</u> offer of guiding the sled. It's not finalized yet, but he put the thought out there.

Definition:_____

_____

10. Terse

Instead of giving a long speech, the principal gave a <u>terse</u> speech.

(Cat video) Snuggles always gives <u>terse</u> responses to any question that is asked. He keeps it brief. He is not the chatterbox like me who goes on and on and on.

Definition:_____

_____

List 2
Part 18

Common ASVAB Vocabulary Words

Transpose to Vindictive

1. Transpose

Children in first grade sometimes <u>transpose</u> letters in the word "from" and spell it "form".

(Cat video) A common spelling error happens when people <u>transpose</u> the letters of a word. Look behind me at the word "from". If you <u>transpose</u> the "r" and "o" in the word from, it becomes the word "form". This is an example of transposing letters.

Definition:_____

_____

2. Unanimous

The jury had a <u>unanimous</u> vote of guilty, where everyone agreed to life in prison for the defendant.

(Cat videos) When I won the championship belt, it was through a <u>unanimous</u> win. Every single judge agreed I was the winner.

Definition:_____

_____

3. Unwieldy

The large umbrella was <u>unwieldy</u> to carry during the windstorm.

(Cat video) Santa carries an <u>unwieldy</u> bag of toys over his shoulder. We are lucky he is strong because that bag is very hard to carry because of its large size.

Definition:_____

_____

4. Vagrant

The <u>vagrant</u> lives in a cardboard box on the corner.

(Cat video) This shopping cart is perfect for a <u>vagrant</u> lifestyle. It would allow me the chance to travel from place to place and beg for a living.

Definition:_____

_____

5. Variable

The wind was <u>variable</u> yesterday and kept changing direction.

(Cat video) The weather is so <u>variable</u> these days. Yesterday it was sunny, and today it is rainy. It is not easy to keep up with this changeable weather.

Definition:_____

_____

6. Vestibule

The bride waited in the <u>vestibule</u> of the church before the walking down the aisle.

(Cat video) I'm expecting a package so I am going to wait right here in the <u>vestibule</u>, inside the front door, right here in the hallway. So when the doorbell rings, I am ready.

Definition:_____

_____

7. Vicious

The guard dog was <u>vicious</u> and attacked anyone who entered the property.

(Cat video) People think I am <u>vicious</u> just because I am wearing a lion's mane, but I am not mean or evil at all. I wouldn't even harm a fly. Umm, but maybe a moth.

Definition:_____

_____

8. Victor

The <u>victor</u> of the fight will win the championship belt.

(Cat video) I train really hard so I make sure that I am the <u>victor</u> of every fight. I win and I win, and I remain the champion.

Definition:_____

_____

9. Vilify

The gossip magazine worked to <u>vilify</u> the politician's reputation with false rumors.

(Cat video) The stories of pirates <u>vilify</u> our names and make us seem like we are all bad people.

Definition:_____

_____

10. Vindictive

Vinny's <u>vindictive</u> ex-girlfriend worked to destroy his reputation after he broke up with her.

(Cat video) At times, criminals can be <u>vindictive</u>. They tend to seek revenge for the people who turned them in.

Definition:_____

_____

List 2
Part 19

Common ASVAB Vocabulary Words

Vital to Zest

1. Vital

Increasing the school budget was a <u>vital</u> part in providing additional services to the students.

(Cat video) A good night's sleep is <u>vital</u> to your health. It is an essential part of life.

Definition:_____

_____

2. Vivid

The primary colors: red, yellow, and blue are <u>vivid</u> colors since they are bright and bold.

(Cat video) I like the <u>vivid</u> colors on my costume. They are lively and colorful.

Definition:_____

_____

3. Volatile

Elvin had a very <u>volatile</u> personality since he could be smiling one minute and threatening others the next.

(Cat video) When I train to go into the ring, I make sure I am ready for <u>volatile</u> opponents. Some of them can be changeable or they can become very violent, but I am ready for them.

Definition:_____

_____

4. Warily

The child walked past the stranger <u>warily</u>, showing caution.

(Cat video) The best advice I can give people is to walk around <u>warily</u>. It is important that you proceed with caution and care when you are out, especially at night.

Definition:_____

_____

5. Wheeze

The asthmatic child started to <u>wheeze</u> during pollen season and needed medication to help him breathe better.

(Cat video) I just came in from chasing a bird, and I am starting to <u>wheeze</u>. I am having a difficult time breathing.

Definition:_____

_____

6. Whim

The young couple was in Vegas and got married on a <u>whim</u>, without even planning it.

(Cat video) I decided to go out for a joyride. It happened on a <u>whim</u>. It was just a sudden, passing idea, but I am having a great time.

Definition:_____

_____

7. Witty

The comedian was very funny and told <u>witty</u> jokes.

(Cat video) I am a <u>witty</u> cat. My jokes are funny in a clever way.

Definition:_____

_____

8. Zest

The 3-year-old girl was so enthusiastic about her friend's birthday that she sang to her with great zest.

(Cat video) I have a zest for boxing. I carry my enthusiasm and my passion into the ring and beyond.

Definition:_____

_____

Common ASVAB Words
Definitions

Part 1
1. Acclaim - approval
2. Acute - sharp, severe
3. Adamant - inflexible
4. Adroit - skillful
5. Aesthetic - having to do with beauty
6. Agile - able to move quickly and easily
7. Ambidextrous - equally skilled in using both hands
8. Ambiguous - not clear in meaning, vague
9. Amenable - agreeable or willing to be influenced or persuaded
10. Amity - peaceful or friendly relations

Part 2
1. Apathy - lack of emotion
2. Appease - to pacify or satisfy by giving into the demands of
3. Apt - quick to learn
4. Aquatic - growing or living in the water
5. Astute - clever or wise
6. Austere - severe
7. Auxiliary - helping
8. Barred - not allowed
9. Belligerent - warlike, ready to fight
10. Benevolent - kind or charitable

Part 3
1. Bland - mild, also meaning lacking in flavor
2. Boggy - wet, soggy (ground)
3. Calligraphy - fancy handwriting
4. Carcass - dead body of an animal
5. Chronic - happening for a long time
6. Compatible - able to get along well together
7. Competent - capable or adequate
8. Complacent - self-satisfied
9. Consequence - the result or effect
10. Corrugated - grooved

Part 4
1. Credible - believable
2. Credulous - believing anything
3. Curt - rudely brief
4. Curtail - to shorten or reduce
5. Debonair - confident, stylish, charming
6. Deft - skilled

7. Defunct - dead or extinct
8. Defy - to oppose something
9. Deplete - to use up
10. Deplore - to be sorry about or to disapprove

Part 5
1. Destitute/Destitution - extreme poverty
2. Diffident - shy
3. Disburse - to pay out
4. Discern - to figure out or recognize
5. Dismay - disappointment
6. Dispel - to scatter or drive away
7. Disperse - to break up or scatter
8. Disrupt - to disturb or interrupt
9. Diverge - to go in different directions
10. Divert - to distract

Part 6
1. Divulge - to reveal
2. Eccentric - odd, unusual
3. Edible - able to be eaten
4. Efface - to erase
5. Eject - to remove
6. Elate - to make happy
7. Eulogy - positive speech about someone usually at a funeral
8. Famish - hungry or starving
9. Feigned - faked
10. Feud - fight

Part 7
1. Fidget - restless or nervous movement
2. Fluorescent - bright light
3. Forlorn - very sad or hopeless
4. Futile - useless
5. Genesis - origin or beginning
6. Germane - relevant, important
7. Glut - too much of something, excess
8. Grating - irritating sound
9. Gratis - free
10. Grim - something unpleasant, depressing or difficult to accept

Part 8
1. Gross - very bad
2. Grotesque - distorted appearance
3. Gruesome - horrible or disgusting
4. Gullible - easily fooled

5. Guttural - harsh sound from deep in the throat
6. Haphazard - random
7. Hardy - strong, bold
8. Hoax - a trick or fraud
9. Hoist - to lift
10. Homogenous - made up of similar parts

Part 9
1. Horrendous - horrible
2. Humid - damp, wet
3. Humorous - funny
4. Illicit - illegal
5. Illusion - a false idea
6. Impromptu - done without preparation
7. Impudent - bold or fearless
8. Incendiary - able to cause a fire or explosion
9. Incinerate - to burn
10. Inclement - rough or stormy

Part 10
1. Indelible - unable to be erased
2. Indifferent - neutral, unconcerned
3. Indispensable - absolutely needed
4. Inept - unfit or unskilled
5. Inertia - an object at rest remains at rest, while an object in motion remains in motion
6. Infallible - unable to make mistakes
7. Infinite - without limits, endless
8. Infinitesimal - very small
9. Ingenious - clever
10. Ingenuous - simple

Part 11
1. Inherent - existing in someone naturally
2. Insipid - uninteresting or boring
3. Instill - to put into
4. Integrity - completeness or honesty
5. Jargon - specialized vocabulary relating to a profession
6. Jeopardy - in danger
7. Jetty - a wall built to protect a harbor
8. Jubilant - joyful
9. Knead - to fold, press or mold dough, clay, etc.
10. Laudable - praiseworthy

Part 12
1. Lethal - deadly
2. Levelheaded - sensible

3. Levity - lightheartedness
4. Limber - flexible
5. Luminous - glowing or shining a bright light
6. Majestic - grand, fancy
7. Malady - illness
8. Malicious - evil
9. Malignant - cancerous
10. Mammoth - very large

Part 13
1. Manual - done by hand
2. Meager - small, inadequate amount
3. Meander - to wander
4. Mercenary - working for money only
5. Meticulous - very exact about details
6. Negligence/Negligent - careless, failing to do the right thing
7. Notary - an official who can certify documents
8. Notorious - famous in a bad way
9. Nullify/Null - to make invalid/invalid
10. Opportune - good timing

Part 14
1. Opulent - very wealthy
2. Panoramic - a wide view in all directions
3. Pensive - thoughtful or reflective
4. Petty - unimportant, small, trivial
5. Picayune - very small, unimportant
6. Posthumous - happening after one's death
7. Potent - powerful
8. Potential - ability
9. Precocious - mature at an early age
10. Prodigious - very large in size, force or extent, enormous

Part 15
1. Profane - disrespect or bad language, swearing
2. Profess - to claim to believe something
3. Prosperous - successful, wealthy
4. Quandary - to be in an uncertain situation, a dilemma
5. Quell - to quiet
6. Rampant - widespread
7. Rescind - to cancel
8. Retaliate/Retaliation - to seek revenge
9. Reticent - unwilling to speak, quiet
10. Rodent - small mammal that gnaws with their teeth, ex: rats, mice

Part 16
1. Satchel - a small bag
2. Scrappy - ready to fight
3. Shrine - a religious site
4. Slander - to speak falsely about another person to ruin their reputation
5. Slender - thin
6. Slovenly - untidy or sloppy
7. Solemn - serious
8. Sophisticated - knowledgeable of the world, not simple
9. Sordid - dirty or wretched
10. Spiritual - relating to the soul or religion

Part 17
1. Sporadic - happening at random
2. Stalwart - strong, sturdy
3. Steadfast - firm, fixed or constant
4. Surmount - to overcome a challenge
5. Tactful/Tact - being able to say the right thing without offending someone
6. Tangible - something you can touch
7. Taut - tightly stretched
8. Tenacious/Tenacity - one who does not give up, persistent
9. Tentative - when something is done but is not final
10. Terse - brief, short

Part 18
1. Transpose - to change the order of
2. Unanimous - all agreeing
3. Unwieldy - hard to carry because large size
4. Vagrant - a person who travels from place to place and begs to make a living
5. Variable - changeable
6. Vestibule - small entrance or hall
7. Vicious - mean or evil
8. Victor - winner
9. Vilify - abusive language
10. Vindictive - seeking revenge

Part 19
1. Vital - essential to life
2. Vivid - lively or colorful
3. Volatile - changeable, threatening to break out in violence
4. Warily - cautiously or carefully
5. Wheeze - difficult breathing with a whistling sound
6. Whim - a sudden, passing idea
7. Witty - funny in a clever way
8. Zest - enthusiasm or passion

Useful ASVAB
Vocabulary Review

List 3
Part 1

Useful ASVAB Vocabulary Words

Abandon to Adhere

1. Abandon

The mother abandoned her children. She left and never came back to care for them.

(Cat video) For some reason, our mother decided to abandon us. We never found out why she decided to give us up without ever planning to come back to us ever again.

Definition:_____

_____

2. Abate

Taking aspirin for a headache can help to abate the pain. It can relieve the suffering by making the pain less.

(Cat video) After a few hours, the storm will abate. When the rain lightens up, we can go out again.

Definition:_____

_____

3. Abet

Lawrence was sent to jail for his decision to <u>abet</u> the bank robber in committing the crime. Helping the robber was considered a crime.

(Cat video) We captured one suspect, and we're on the search for the other. We're on the search for the one who decided to <u>abet</u> him in committing his crime. He encouraged him and helped him by driving the getaway car.

Definition:_____

_____

4. Abolish

The king did not agree with slavery, so he decided to <u>abolish</u> it.

(Cat video) When I became king, I decided to <u>abolish</u> rules that I did not agree with. As king, I had the authority to do away with these rules.

Definition:_____

_____

5. Abort

The military leader told his troops to <u>abort</u> the mission. They needed to cut the mission short because it became too dangerous to continue.

(Cat video) On one of my last rescues, I was told by my captain to <u>abort</u> the mission. He told me to cut it short and not proceed in searching the building because it was too dangerous to continue.

Definition:_____

_____

6. Abridge

The author decided to <u>abridge</u> his book because it was too long.

(Cat video) I decided to <u>abridge</u> the book I wrote. It was too long, so I shortened it.

Definition:_____

_____

7. Abstain

In becoming a vegetarian, Marjorie will <u>abstain</u> from eating meat.

(Cat video) Before a big boxing match, I decide to <u>abstain</u> from sugar. I voluntarily give up all sweets so my body can be in the best possible shape it can be.

Definition:_____

_____

8. Acumen

The businessman had great <u>acumen</u> when it came to investing money and was admired for his sharpness of mind.

(Cat video) I have built my business through my <u>acumen</u>. My sharpness of mind and my keen sense of business have helped me greatly.

Definition:_____

_____

9. Adequate

Timothy cooked an <u>adequate</u> amount of food for his party. There was enough food for everyone invited.

(Cat video) I forgot my umbrella today, but I am sure my rain gear will be <u>adequate</u> to keep me dry. I think this will be enough. It should be satisfactory for today.

Definition:_____

_____

10. Adhere

In order to continue living in the dorm at school, the students must <u>adhere</u> to the rules. Following the dorm rules will allow them to continue residing there.

(Cat video) We will <u>adhere</u> to our plan to remodel this home. This is a plan we will hold onto.

Definition:_____

_____

List 3
Part 2

Useful ASVAB Vocabulary Words

Adjourn to Assess

1. Adjourn

The court case will <u>adjourn</u> at 4:00 PM today, and will resume tomorrow at 9:00 AM.

(Cat video) We will <u>adjourn</u> our meeting at 5PM. That will end our meeting for today, and we will continue tomorrow.

Definition:_____

_____

2. Adversary

Not everyone is our friend. Sometimes we meet an <u>adversary</u>, or an enemy.

(Cat video) I am dressed in armor, so I am ready to meet my <u>adversary</u>. We must remain safe while we are trying to battle our enemies.

Definition:_____

_____

3. Advocate

Shana is an animal rights <u>advocate</u> who speaks in the support of the prevention of animal abuse.

(Cat video) I consider myself an animal rights <u>advocate</u>. I plead for and urge for the protection of animals.

Definition:_____

_____

4. Agitate

Waiting in the doctor's office for test results tends to <u>agitate</u> some people making them very nervous.

(Cat video) Being stuck in traffic tends to <u>agitate</u> me. It really disturbs me.

Definition:_____

_____

5. Allude

The politician <u>alluded</u> to the fact that she would run for office and hinted at her desire to be a Senator.

(Cat video) By wearing this costume, I am trying to <u>allude</u> to the fact that I would enjoy a home cooked meal. I hope my owner catches on to the hint.

Definition:_____

_____

6. Aloof

The girl was considered <u>aloof</u> because she was distant when others would speak to her.

(Cat video) People often refer to Snuggles as <u>aloof</u>. They think he is a little distant, reserved or even cold in his mannerisms.

Definition:_____

_____

7. Amicable

The two countries had <u>amicable</u> relations, and their conferences were always held in a friendly and peaceful manner.

(Cat video) The dogs and I have an <u>amicable</u> relationship. Even though people think cats and dogs can't get along, we are very friendly toward each other.

Definition:_____

_____

8. Anomaly

Having six fingers on one hand is considered an <u>anomaly</u>. This abnormality is found in some people around the world.

(Cat video) Being a toilet-trained cat is somewhat of an <u>anomaly</u> in the cat world. It definitely is an abnormality and an irregularity from what people normally see cats doing.

Definition:_____

_____

9. Assert

The shy little girl needed to <u>assert</u> herself. She needed to learn to speak confidently.

(Cat video) It is important to be able to <u>assert</u> yourself in life. It's a good thing to claim or state positively what you want out of life.

Definition:_____

_____

10. Assess

The realtor will <u>assess</u> the value of the house and decide on the selling price.

(Cat video) Before this house is sold, they will need to <u>assess</u> it. When they do that, they will decide upon its value.

Definition:_____

_____

List 3
Part 3

Useful ASVAB Vocabulary Words

Attain to Capricious

1. Attain

Working hard helps people <u>attain</u> their goals because gains come from work.

(Cat video) I have <u>attained</u> much success as a trumpet player. I have obtained or reached this goal because of all my practice.

Definition:_____

_____

2. Atypical

Bradley's blood test results were <u>atypical</u>. As a result, he needed to meet with the doctor to discuss his abnormal test results.

(Cat video) People consider me an <u>atypical</u> cat. I take that as a compliment. I like being considered abnormal or unusual.

Definition:_____

_____

3. Baffle

The logic puzzle was able to <u>baffle</u> many minds, even the smartest students were confused by it.

(Cat video) As a superhero, I work to <u>baffle</u> the villains. I confuse, perplex, or frustrate them so they cannot defeat me.

Definition:_____

_____

4. Banal

The expression "it is what it is" is such a <u>banal</u> expression. It is totally overused and lacking in originality.

(Cat video) Some expressions are so <u>banal</u> like the one, "it's raining cats and dogs". Such a commonplace expression. It's a bit overused if you ask me.

Definition:_____

_____

5. Barren

The desert is a <u>barren</u> place. Very few plants grow there.

(Cat video) Cactus can grow in a <u>barren</u> environment. Even though the desert is unfruitful and unproductive, it doesn't stop the cactus from growing.

Definition:_____

_____

6. Belie

The smile on William's face <u>belied</u> the cruel look in his eyes and disguised his mean intentions.

(Cat video) Do not let my appearance <u>belie</u> who I am. Even though I appear to be mean, under all this, I am a real pussycat.

Definition:_____

_____

7. Bogus

Caroline thought she bought a designer bag, but it turned out to be a <u>bogus</u> one, not a genuine designer bag.

(Cat video) We found a suspect who made a purchase with a <u>bogus</u> $100 bill. We are very strict with people who use counterfeit money, and we are not happy to see this fake money in circulation.

Definition:_____

_____

8. Boycott

The animal rights group encourages people to <u>boycott</u> companies that take part in animal testing. Deciding to not use or buy their products would support the cause to end animal testing.

(Cat video) I have decided to <u>boycott</u> companies that take part in animal testing. I simply refuse to use products from companies that could hurt animals.

Definition:_____

_____

9. Candid

Ron was very <u>candid</u> about his past. He did not keep any secrets, but was very honest and open.

(Cat video) I've always been known for being <u>candid</u>. I just tell it like it is. I am very honest and open.

Definition:_____

_____

10. Capricious

Due to Ted's <u>capricious</u> nature, no one could rely on him for a final answer. His ideas always changed suddenly and without warning.

(Cat video) I am known for being <u>capricious</u>. I change my mind very easily and without warning.

Definition:_____

_____

List 3
Part 4

Useful ASVAB Vocabulary Words

Chaos to Compromise

1. Chaos

At the scene of the accident, there was much <u>chaos</u>. The police needed to control the confusion and disorder.

(Cat video) When we arrived at the scene of the fire, there was complete <u>chaos</u>. People were running and screaming. There was much confusion and much disorder.

Definition:_____

_____

2. Clandestine

The group held <u>clandestine</u> meetings that were secret from many.

(Cat video) We found out about the <u>clandestine</u> meetings the dog owners were having. They were making secret plans about dogfights, but we stopped it before it became a problem.

Definition:_____

_____

3. Coerce

The bank robber planned to <u>coerce</u> the teller to give him the money. He would force her to hand over the money.

(Cat video) We just arrested a man who decided to <u>coerce</u> an elderly woman into giving him her money. He forced her to hand over her pocketbook to him.

Definition:_____

_____

4. Cogent

The lawyer made a <u>cogent</u> argument for his client. His argument was clear and convincing.

(Cat video) I make a <u>cogent</u> argument for the advancement of animal rights. Let me tell you, I can be pretty convincing when I want to be.

Definition:_____

_____

5. Coherent

The lawyer made a <u>coherent</u> argument for his client. He spoke in a logical and consistent way that was understood by all.

(Cat video) When I give a speech, I make sure it is <u>coherent</u>. It needs to be logically connected and organized.

Definition:_____

_____

6. Collaborate

The band will <u>collaborate</u> to write a new song. When they work together, they create the best songs.

(Cat video) On the construction site, it is very important that the other coworkers and I <u>collaborate</u>. We need to work together on this project to make sure we meet the deadline.

Definition:_____

_____

7. Colleague

When a person starts a new job, it is useful to learn from <u>colleagues</u>. Other workers in the same profession have much knowledge from experience and are willing to give advice.

(Cat video) You can learn a lot from a <u>colleague</u> in the workplace. It's important to see what lessons can be learned from fellow workers in the same profession as you.

Definition:_____

_____

8. Comparable

The climate of Seattle, Washington is <u>comparable</u> to the climate of Ireland, with many mild damp days.

(Cat video) In all his long years, Santa never could find another reindeer that was <u>comparable</u> to me. Even though he searched, he never found one that was equal or worthy to be compared to me with my shiny nose.

Definition:_____

_____

9. Compose

The songwriter decided to <u>compose</u> a new song since she enjoyed creating her own music.

(Cat video) I like to <u>compose</u> my own music. I put together some great songs that I can play on my guitar.

Definition:_____

_____

10. Compromise

Instead of going to war, the two countries that were disagreeing came to a <u>compromise</u> over the issue at hand. Each side made an agreement in which they gave up something they wanted to ensure peace.

(Cat video) To end disagreements, both sides need to come to a <u>compromise</u>. This is where they find a settlement in which both sides give up something.

Definition:_____

_____

List 3
Part 5

Useful ASVAB Vocabulary Words

Concede to Covert

1. Concede

The mayor will <u>concede</u> to his opponent in the election. He is giving in that he lost to his opponent.

(Cat video) The enemy will <u>concede</u> to our demands. They will yield to what is right when we are through with them.

Definition:_____

_____

2. Concept

The teacher will introduce a new <u>concept</u> in math class today, and the students will work on the new idea.

(Cat video) I have to give a lot of credit to the person who came up with the <u>concept</u> of a raincoat. What a great idea! I mean, it keeps you dry in the rain.

Definition:_____

_____

3. Concise

Book reviews are meant to be <u>concise</u>. They are kept brief, not long.

(Cat video) When I speak, I like to be <u>concise</u>. I choose to be brief and to the point.

Definition:_____

_____

4. Conduct

In school, students are rewarded for good <u>conduct</u> since proper behavior is an important part of their education.

(Cat video) Prisoners are released early at times based on their <u>conduct</u>. Good behavior often equals an early release.

Definition:_____

_____

5. Confidential

The documents contained <u>confidential</u> information and needed to be kept secret.

(Cat video) When work memos are marked <u>confidential</u>, it is very important to make sure they remain private or secret.

Definition:_____

_____

6. Conscientious

Jackson is a <u>conscientious</u> student who always works to the best of his ability.

(Cat video) I have always been a <u>conscientious</u> student. I am faithful to my work or to doing what is right.

Definition:_____

_____

7. Consume

In three days, the family <u>consumed</u> all the groceries. They needed to go shopping since they used up all the food they had.

(Cat video) When I am in workout mode, I <u>consume</u> much more food. I use up more food to keep up my energy.

Definition:_____

_____

8. Contaminate

Wash your hands before cooking so you do not <u>contaminate</u> the food. Cooking with dirty hands can make your food unclean or unsafe.

(Cat video) Before surgery, we wash our hands thoroughly so we do not <u>contaminate</u> the operating room with germs. We make sure that we do not pollute or make it unclean or unfit for our patients.

Definition:_____

_____

9. Contempt

Scott feels <u>contempt</u> for the man who robbed his house and views him as worthless.

(Cat video) I have a great deal of <u>contempt</u> for my enemies. I feel strong dislike and disapproval for their actions.

Definition:_____

_____

10. Covert

The spy had many <u>covert</u> missions, which he kept secret from everyone.

(Cat video) The police set up a task force who ran a <u>covert</u> operation to find the suspects. It was a secret and hidden operation that no one knew about.

Definition:_____

_____

List 3
Part 6

Useful ASVAB Vocabulary Words

Creed to Demolish

1. Creed

Many churches have a <u>creed</u> that people recite in which they state their religious beliefs in a prayer.

(Cat video) As an angel, I know that a <u>creed</u> is a statement of one's faith or beliefs.

Definition:_____

_____

2. Culpable

The child was <u>culpable</u> for stealing the cookies from the cookie jar. His mother saw him do it and knew he was to blame.

(Cat video) After confronting the suspect, we realized he was <u>culpable</u>. He had confessed to the crime so we knew he was the guilty party.

Definition:_____

_____

3. Dearth

The desert has so little rainfall that it has a <u>dearth</u> of water.

(Cat video) As homeless kittens, there was a <u>dearth</u> of food and water for us to live on. There was much lack and scarcity in our conditions.

Definition:_____

_____

4. Debilitate

Cancer can <u>debilitate</u> a person. It is one of many diseases that can weaken a person.

(Cat video) When I meet my opponent, part of my goal is to <u>debilitate</u> him. I want to weaken him to the point where he cannot fight back, and I can keep my belt.

Definition:_____

_____

5. Deceive

The used car salesman worked to <u>deceive</u> the customer by telling her the car was in perfect running condition when it really had a faulty transmission. He was trying to mislead her so she would buy the car.

(Cat video) Pirates <u>deceive</u> others. We work very hard to trick and lie in our lives.

Definition:_____

_____

6. Decimate

The bomb <u>decimated</u> almost the entire town, and most of the people of that town were killed.

(Cat video) A natural part of being a cat is the desire to <u>decimate</u> the bird population. I can't help wanting to destroy all the birds in town.

Definition:_____

_____

7. Decrepit

The <u>decrepit</u> building needed to be destroyed. It was so worn out by old age that it was beyond repair.

(Cat video) We determined that the <u>decrepit</u> building was unfit to live in. It had been broken down by old age, and no one should reside there.

Definition:_____

_____

8. Delete

When I make a mistake in my typing, I decide to <u>delete</u> it. When I turn in my final work, I make sure there are no mistakes.

(Cat video) I make sure to <u>delete</u> junk emails. It's important to erase them that way my inbox isn't overloaded.

Definition:_____

_____

9. Demolish

The construction crew needed to <u>demolish</u> the building. It was in very bad repair and needed to be destroyed.

(Cat video) After the fire, the owners of the building decided they had to <u>demolish</u> the building. It could not be repaired. Instead, it had to be destroyed completely.

Definition:_____

_____

Julie A. Hyers © 2020

List 3
Part 7

Useful ASVAB Vocabulary Words

Demote to Docile

1. Demote

Due to his poor work performance, Nathan was <u>demoted</u> to a lower job position that paid less.

(Cat video) I need to <u>demote</u> one of my employees today. He will be given a lower rank in the job site because he has not been effective in his work.

Definition:_____

_____

2. Deprive

Samuel knew that working such long hours would <u>deprive</u> him of sleep. Many good nights' sleep had been taken from him because of work.

(Cat video) Some people are very cruel when they <u>deprive</u> animals of their food. It is wrong to take away food from an animal.

Definition:_____

_____

3. Detrimental

The hurricane was <u>detrimental</u> to the homes on the island. It caused great damage.

(Cat video) It is a well-known fact that smoking cigarettes is <u>detrimental</u> to your health. It causes damage or harm.

Definition:_____

_____

4. Deviation

Talking to yourself is considered a <u>deviation</u> from normal. It is not a commonly accepted behavior.

(Cat video) A cat driving a car is truly a <u>deviation</u> from normal. It is different from the usual or common way a cat behaves.

Definition:_____

_____

5. Diminish

At first, Lisa was very sick from her medicine, but after a few days her side effects started to <u>diminish</u>. She was happy that her side effects were becoming less.

(Cat video) Since I have been spending so much money, my savings are starting <u>diminish</u>. They are becoming less.

Definition:_____

_____

6. Discard

We were reminded to <u>discard</u> our garbage before leaving the train. Getting rid of the garbage before getting off the train is one way to keep the train cleaner.

(Cat video) I plan to <u>discard</u> this green wig. I'm thinking of throwing it out because it really doesn't suit me.

Definition:_____

_____

7. Disclose

The news program will <u>disclose</u> the identity of the bank robber on the 6 PM news. This is when his name will be revealed.

(Cat video) A person was hit by a car downtown. We have not yet <u>disclosed</u> their identity. We will reveal who it was later on today.

Definition:_____

_____

133

8. Dismal

Before the storm, the black clouds were <u>dismal</u>. Their dark and gloomy appearance warned that the storm was near.

(Cat video) After Fluffy's operation, we told his friends the <u>dismal</u> news that he would not survive his diagnosis. It was gloomy and dreary news for them.

Definition:_____

_____

9. Diverse

The city's schools consist of a <u>diverse</u> population. The students come from varied backgrounds.

(Cat video) I have a very <u>diverse</u> group of friends. They are a varied group, and none are like each other.

Definition:_____

_____

10. Docile

Beagles are considered a <u>docile</u> dog breed since they are easy to train.

(Cat video) My owner thinks that just because she dresses me up like a sheep that I am going to become a <u>docile</u> animal. Well, it never going to happen. I will never be easily led, no matter what I am wearing.

Definition:_____

_____

List 3
Part 8

Useful ASVAB Vocabulary Words

Dormant to Enlightened

1. Dormant

The groundhog is <u>dormant</u> for the winter, and he wakes up in the spring.

(Cat video) Today I have entered into a <u>dormant</u> state. I have been sleeping and inactive all day.

Definition:_____

_____

2. Dubious

Steven told the police that did not steal the car, but the police were <u>dubious</u> about his story. They had their doubts.

(Cat video) I am <u>dubious</u> about the cause of the fire. It was said to be accidental, but I have my doubts.

Definition:_____

_____

3. Durable

When buying a folder, it is a good idea to buy a <u>durable</u> one that is strong enough to last for a long time.

(Cat video) I built this house myself. I needed to make sure it is <u>durable</u> because it needs to be tough and long lasting.

Definition:_____

_____

135

4. Dwindle

After retiring, Dominic's savings began to <u>dwindle</u> since he was spending more than he was earning.

(Cat video) I've been spending money so quickly that my savings are starting to <u>dwindle</u>. They're becoming less and less.

Definition:_____

_____

5. Eclectic

Vance had an <u>eclectic</u> music selection. He enjoyed a great variety of music from a wide range of artists that spanned over many decades.

(Cat video) I like to believe I have an <u>eclectic</u> style when it comes to fashion. You see the various accessories I am wearing? They came from very diverse sources. Some came from doll's outfits, human outfits, and dog outfits. Makes me who I am!

Definition:_____

_____

6. Elusive

Some people consider the bald eagle to be and <u>elusive</u> bird. It is often difficult to find.

(Cat video) Many view happiness as <u>elusive</u>. It is hard to define and hard to grasp.

Definition:_____

_____

7. Empathy

Showing <u>empathy</u> for others is a sign of being a caring person. It enables one to share in another's emotions, thoughts or feelings.

(Cat video) It is important as part of the medical staff to be able to provide <u>empathy</u> for patients. In having empathy, you are able to identify with what the other person is feeling.

Definition:_____

_____

8. Enable

Annette's scholarship will <u>enable</u> her to go to college for free. Her scholarship is making it possible for her to advance her education.

(Cat video) Education helps to <u>enable</u> people to help escape poverty. Having a good education makes this possible because people have more opportunities.

Definition:_____

_____

9. Enhance

Many women feel that wearing makeup will <u>enhance</u> their appearance. They count on makeup to make them look better.

(Cat video) Taking proper care of myself allows me to <u>enhance</u> by appearance. I do believe it definitely improves how I look.

Definition:_____

_____

10. Enlightened

The <u>enlightened</u> person is aware of the world around them lives a life free from ignorance and prejudice.

(Cat video) As an angel, I feel I am <u>enlightened</u>. I am free from being ignorant and prejudiced, and I am socially and intellectually advanced.

Definition:_____

_____

List 3
Part 9

Useful ASVAB Vocabulary Words

Entitle to Fallacious

1. Entitle

Winning the beauty pageant will <u>entitle</u> the young lady with the title of Miss America. She will then have claim to that title for a year.

(Cat video) Earning the most touchdowns in a football season often will <u>entitle</u> someone to the award of MVP, most valuable player. This will give them the right or claim to that award.

Definition:_____

_____

2. Equivocal

The politician gave an <u>equivocal</u> response to the question. He purposely remained unclear in his response.

(Cat video) What should I do if one day, the girl I propose to gives me an <u>equivocal</u> response? There is nothing worse than an unclear or uncertain response to a question like that!

Definition:_____

_____

3. Evaluate

The jeweler will <u>evaluate</u> the diamond to determine its value.

(Cat video) In applying for scholarships, the schools needed to <u>evaluate</u> my grades. They needed to determine if I was worthy of receiving a scholarship.

Definition:_____

_____

4. Evasive

Catherine is <u>evasive</u> in discussing which candidate she plans to vote for in the election. She avoids the topic every time it comes up.

(Cat video) The politician was <u>evasive</u> when questioned about his plans to run for re-election. He avoided answering the question when asked.

Definition:_____

_____

5. Evoke

Looking at pictures from childhood will <u>evoke</u> certain memories. These pictures call forth certain thoughts into one's mind.

(Cat video) Thinking about the loss of Fluffy <u>evokes</u> many feelings. When I think about the friend I lost, lots of feelings are stirred up within me.

Definition:_____

_____

6. Expel

The principal decided to <u>expel</u> the student for his poor behavior. He was removed from the school and not allowed to return.

(Cat video) As a high school principal, there were a number of students that I needed to <u>expel</u> because of their poor behavior. They were forced out of the school.

Definition:_____

_____

7. Exploit

Underpaying employees is one way that employers can <u>exploit</u> their employees. They are using them selfishly for profit.

(Cat video) Animal testing is one way that people <u>exploit</u> animals. This is an unfair or selfish use of animals.

Definition:_____

_____

8. Extraneous

When Maria wrote her research paper, she needed to make sure she did not include any extraneous information. She needed to avoid including any irrelevant or unrelated materials.

(Cat video) As a cat, eating human food is extraneous for me. It is not essential, but I sure do enjoy it.

Definition:_____

_____

9. Facetious

Sharon was facetious at her mother's funeral, making jokes at such an inappropriate time.

(Cat video) Sometimes I get accused of being facetious. I will admit, sometimes I do joke at inappropriate times.

Definition:_____

_____

10. Fallacious

The man was convicted based on fallacious evidence. Years later, the courts realized that he served prison time for mistaken beliefs on the part of the court.

(Cat video) It is fallacious to believe that just because something is popular that it is right. This is a mistaken belief.

Definition:_____

_____

List 3
Part 10

Useful ASVAB Vocabulary Words

Feasible to Harass

1. Feasible

Finishing a bachelor's degree in less than 4 years is <u>feasible</u> if summer classes are taken. With some extra work, it is capable of being done.

(Cat video) Preparing for a dinner party for 20 people for tomorrow night is a <u>feasible</u> act for me. I am sure that I'll be able to perform this.

Definition:_____

_____

2. Fickle

Bert was very <u>fickle</u> when it came to his taste in food. One day, he loved a certain meal, and the next day, he hated it. He was very unpredictable.

(Cat video) Some people are <u>fickle</u> with how they like to eat their hot dogs. One day, they might like ketchup. Next day, they might like mustard. Fickle people change their minds quite easily.

Definition:_____

_____

3. Forfeit

If Rachel did not finish her vegetables, she would <u>forfeit</u> the right to watch television. Her mother took away her right to watch television whenever she did not do as she was told.

(Cat video) In one match, my opponent decided to <u>forfeit</u>. He lost because of his actions of leaving the ring.

Definition:_____

_____

4. Fortuitous

Winning the basket at the raffle was a <u>fortuitous</u> event. It happened by luck.

(Cat video) Winning the lottery was a <u>fortuitous</u> event for me. It happened by pure luck.

Definition:_____

_____

5. Fraudulent

The man took part in <u>fraudulent</u> behavior, tricking others by pretending to be a medical doctor.

(Cat video) We found the suspect who was accused of <u>fraudulent</u> use of a credit card. He had stolen someone else's card and was using it falsely and making purchases of which the owner did not approve.

Definition:_____

_____

6. Fundamental

The constitution was written to provide the American people with <u>fundamental</u> rights. It ensures that their basic rights are protected.

(Cat video) When you make it to basic training or boot camp, this is where you learn the <u>fundamental</u> policies of the military. You learn the basic things and start from there and build upon it.

Definition:_____

_____

7. Gracious

It was very <u>gracious</u> of Samantha to offer to host dinner for everyone. Her kindness was much appreciated by all.

(Cat video) My owner was <u>gracious</u> enough to give me this lovely stroller. That was so courteous and kind of her.

Definition:_____

_____

8. Gregarious

Salvatore was known for his <u>gregarious</u> nature. He had always been sociable and loved the company of others.

(Cat video) I'm very <u>gregarious</u>. I love socializing and spending time with friends.

Definition:_____

_____

9. Guile

Foxes are known for their <u>guile</u> in many children's stories. They are often shown as being sly and tricky.

(Cat video) As a pirate, I use my <u>guile</u> to gain my riches. It is all based on my cunning and my deceit. That's how I gain my wealth.

Definition:_____

_____

10. Harass

The bully did <u>harass</u> the weakest child in the class. She made repeated attacks against her.

(Cat video) As pirates, we <u>harass</u> people on the high seas. We annoy them with our repeated attacks until we get what we want.

Definition:_____

_____

List 3
Part 11

Useful ASVAB Vocabulary Words

Hectic to Indigenous

1. Hectic

The city is a very <u>hectic</u> place, full of activity and very busy.

(Cat video) The construction site can become a <u>hectic</u> place. There's a lot going on, and it can become very hurried and confused if order is not established.

Definition:_____

_____

2. Hinder

Being in a wheelchair would <u>hinder</u> Renee's ability to take part in some sports. It could hold her back from being active in these sports.

(Cat video) This outfit will <u>hinder</u> my ability to get around. It definitely prevents me from moving forward.

Definition:_____

_____

3. Illusion

Some people are under the <u>illusion</u> that success can happen without hard work, but that is just a false idea.

(Cat video) I know you might think that what you are looking at is an <u>illusion</u>. But I assure you this is not a false appearance or a misleading vision. You are looking at a cat who is an angel, when I am not stealing food off the table of course that is.

Definition:_____

_____

4. Immune

Vaccines help to make people <u>immune</u> from diseases so they are protected from catching them.

(Cat video) In the medical field, we like to give people vaccines to make sure they are <u>immune</u> to certain diseases. These shots help to protect them from getting the disease.

Definition:_____

_____

5. Impartial

A judge needs to be <u>impartial</u> in hearing a case. It is important to be able to make a fair judgment.

(Cat video) It's very important in boxing to have <u>impartial</u> judges because if the judges are fair, you know the match will be decided properly.

Definition:_____

_____

6. Impeccable

With her makeup on, Georgia had an <u>impeccable</u> look. Her skin was flawless.

(Cat video) It isn't easy to have an <u>impeccable</u> appearance. That's why it takes a lot of time for me to get my flawless look.

Definition:_____

_____

7. Imply

The husband did not directly tell his wife he did not like her outfit. He simply <u>implied</u> that his wife's outfit was not acceptable when he said, "You are not going to wear that. Are you?"

(Cat video) Instead of stating something directly, sometimes I just <u>imply</u> things and give people hints.

Definition:_____

_____

8. Impressive

Doug bought an <u>impressive</u> car to attract the admiration of others.

(Cat video) This engagement ring I picked out is pretty <u>impressive</u>. I think it will attract a lot of attention.

Definition:_____

_____

9. Inception

Max lived in the same town from the <u>inception</u> of his life to the very end.

(Cat video) From the very <u>inception</u> of the life of our home in our human family, we knew we were wanted. We knew it from the very beginning.

Definition:_____

_____

10. Indigenous

The American bison is an animal that is <u>indigenous</u> to North America. This is its native habitat where it naturally exists.

(Cat video) These animals are all <u>indigenous</u> to North America. That means they're naturally found there. That's just where they're from.

Definition:_____

_____

List 3
Part 12

Useful ASVAB Vocabulary Words

Induct to Lament

1. Induct

The baseball hall of fame will <u>induct</u> new members into its group this year. Each year new people are admitted into this organization.

(Cat video) I was a good student so they decided to <u>induct</u> me into the honor society. I was brought into this group because of my high grades.

Definition:_____

_____

2. Inferior

A silver medal is <u>inferior</u> to a gold medal. It is lower in rank.

(Cat video) I love being a superhero. This way I don't feel <u>inferior</u> to anyone. I am not of lower degree or poorer quality than anyone around me.

Definition:_____

_____

3. Initiate

The president of the board decided to <u>initiate</u> the meeting. He started the meeting as soon as everyone involved had arrived.

(Cat video) Today we will <u>initiate</u> repairs on this home. We will begin them shortly.

Definition:_____

_____

4. Innocuous

The mother was happy to find out that her baby's virus was <u>innocuous</u>. His harmless virus would pass in a few days with no long-lasting effects.

(Cat video) I might look harmful, but I am completely <u>innocuous</u>. As harmless as can be!

Definition:_____

_____

5. Innovation

Over the last century there have been many <u>innovations</u> in the field of technology. Advancements are happening each and every day.

(Cat video) Being taught vocabulary by a cat is an <u>innovation</u>. This is something new. It's a change in method or custom of how things are previously done.

Definition:_____

_____

6. Instinct

Cats are born with an <u>instinct</u> to hunt. It is a natural tendency they have from birth.

(Cat video) My desire to chase birds is an <u>instinct</u>. It's just a natural feeling that comes with being a cat.

Definition:_____

_____

7. Intuition

Some people rely on <u>intuition</u> to make judgments about life's situations. They depend on knowledge that they have without any proof. It is more of a gut feeling upon which they depend.

(Cat video) When I meet people, I rely on my <u>intuition</u> to tell me what kind of people they are. I have this gut feeling. It's a natural instinct, and I can tell good people from bad people.

Definition:_____

_____

8. Irate

When Tyrone found his car window had been smashed in, he was <u>irate</u>. He was extremely angry to be the victim of such a crime.

(Cat video) When I found out the enemy had invaded our territory, I was <u>irate</u>. It's been a long time since I was as intensely angry as this.

Definition:_____

_____

9. Itinerary

Cody has the <u>itinerary</u> planned for his trip. His schedule is very busy.

(Cat video) I'm going on tour with the orchestra, and I just received a copy of the <u>itinerary</u>. The plan or schedule of travel looks very busy. It's very exciting.

Definition:_____

_____

10. Lament

The widow needed to <u>lament</u> over the loss of her husband. She was left deeply sorrowful and needed time to mourn.

(Cat video) Some days I sit around, and I <u>lament</u> over the loss of Fluffy. There are days I just need to mourn over him.

Definition:_____

_____

List 3
Part 13

Useful ASVAB Vocabulary Words

Legible to Mediocre

1. Legible

My handwriting is always <u>legible</u>. People can always read my writing.

(Cat video) When I handwrite a memo at work, I make sure its is <u>legible</u>. It is very important that it is written clearly and able to be read.

Definition:_____

_____

2. Leisurely

Ingrid completed her homework at a <u>leisurely</u> pace. She was in no rush to complete it.

(Cat video) I'm just about to settle down for a nice, long <u>leisurely</u> nap. I'll take my time and relax. I'm in no rush to get up.

Definition:_____

_____

3. Lethargic

During the heat wave, Sara felt so <u>lethargic</u> that all she wanted to do was lay around and rest.

(Cat video) It's morning time. Time to get up, but I am feeling so <u>lethargic</u>. I am so drowsy and sleepy this morning. I wish I could sleep all day.

Definition:_____

_____

4. Lithe

The ballerina has a <u>lithe</u>, agile body allowing her to do very flexible moves in her dancing.

(Cat video) I have been chosen as an aerobics instructor because I am so <u>lithe</u>. It isn't easy being so gracefully flexible, but it has its benefits.

Definition:_____

_____

5. Loathe

Many animal rights activists <u>loathe</u> the act of the creation of fur coats. They have intense hatred for the act of killing animals for their fur.

(Cat video) As a superhero, I <u>loathe</u> villains. I have a strong dislike and disgust for the bad guys.

Definition:_____

_____

6. Lucid

Paul had a <u>lucid</u> dream that was very clear and easily understood.

(Cat video) When teaching others, it is important to use <u>lucid</u> explanations. Clear explanations help the learning process.

Definition:_____

_____

7. Lucrative

Certain occupations are very <u>lucrative</u>, leaving people with a great amount of wealth.

(Cat video) I am fortunate to have entered into a <u>lucrative</u> field. The line of work I am in is very profitable, and I am able to have my own money.

Definition:_____

_____

8. Magnitude

The <u>magnitude</u> of the forest fire was enormous, and it affected people to a great extent.

(Cat video) We recently fought a terrible fire. We did not realize the <u>magnitude</u> of this fire until we arrived at the scene, and when we got there, we saw its true size.

Definition:_____

_____

9. Malleable

Many types of metal are <u>malleable</u> and can be molded and shaped without breaking.

(Cat video) The armor that I am wearing is a <u>malleable</u> type of substance. It was able to be shaped to suit my size and figure.

Definition:_____

_____

10. Mediocre

Deirdre was taught to never settle for being <u>mediocre</u>. She knew that being ordinary or average was not good enough for her.

(Cat video) No one wants to be a <u>mediocre</u> football player. Who wants to be average when you can strive to be the best?

Definition:_____

_____

List 3
Part 14

Useful ASVAB Vocabulary Words

Mend to Nascent

1. Mend

Mary knew how to <u>mend</u> the holes in her socks. Her mother taught her how to repair holes in her clothes at a young age.

(Cat video) My job today is to <u>mend</u> a broken fence. I'm going to correct the problem, and I will improve upon it.

Definition:_____

_____

2. Meritorious

Winning a gold medal in gymnastics was a <u>meritorious</u> achievement for Brittany. This was an achievement that was worthy of praise.

(Cat video) Earning my degree was the most <u>meritorious</u> achievement of my life. It was definitely worthy of praise and reward.

Definition:_____

_____

3. Minute

When Sharon went to the concert, she came home and told her sister every <u>minute</u> detail of the night. She mentioned even the smallest details of her night out.

(Cat video) There is a <u>minute</u> detail that is keeping me from resting peacefully. And that is, the lights are still on. I know it is a small detail, but please.

Definition:_____

_____

153

4. Misnomer

Calling a peanut a nut is a <u>misnomer</u>. It is the wrong name to use since peanuts are not nuts at all, but legumes.

(Cat video) When it comes to cats, the term declawing is actually a <u>misnomer</u>. The proper term is actually bone amputation. So, do not let this inaccurate term fool you.

Definition:_____

_____

5. Mitigate

The judge decided to <u>mitigate</u> the criminal's prison sentence. He made it less severe because it was his first offense.

(Cat video) At the trial, the lawyer fought to <u>mitigate</u> the charges against her client. She tried to make the charges less severe.

Definition:_____

_____

6. Morose

When Evan found out the <u>morose</u> news that his friend was dying, it left him in a gloomy mood.

(Cat video) Talking about the loss of Fluffy puts me in a <u>morose</u> mood. It always makes me feel so gloomy and sulky.

Definition:_____

_____

7. Motivation

Terry's desire to help people was the reason behind her <u>motivation</u> to become a nurse.

(Cat video) <u>Motivation</u> is a key part in being able to finish school. When you have motivation, you have a strong reason for doing something.

Definition:_____

_____

8. Mundane

Life is filled with <u>mundane</u> tasks like putting out the garbage, cleaning, and organizing. People must complete many ordinary tasks in life.

(Cat video) Life is made up of many <u>mundane</u> tasks. Lots of things we do in life are very unexciting, everyday tasks like putting away the laundry.

Definition:_____

_____

9. Naïve

Children are often <u>naïve</u> and are easily fooled. They are quick to believe what people tell them.

(Cat video) As kittens, we were <u>naïve</u>. We were unsophisticated and not very knowledgeable about the world.

Definition:_____

_____

10. Nascent

Back in the 1980s, the use of computers in school was a <u>nascent</u> idea. Today computer use in schools is far more advanced that those beginning years.

(Cat video) I will always remember my first days of my <u>nascent</u> pro-football career. Scoring the first touchdown of my football career was an amazing achievement for me.

Definition:_____

_____

List 3
Part 15

Useful ASVAB Vocabulary Words

Neglectful to Obtuse

1. Neglectful

Some pet owners are <u>neglectful</u> and do not provide for their pet's basic needs.

(Cat video) Our mother was very <u>neglectful</u>. She was careless and heedless. She didn't even make sure we had food to eat.

Definition:_____

_____

2. Nonchalant

Even though her nursing exam was tomorrow, Marie had a <u>nonchalant</u> attitude and remained calm and relaxed.

(Cat video) I like to keep a <u>nonchalant</u> attitude in life. That way, I am cool and unconcerned, and I don't really get too bothered over things.

Definition:_____

_____

3. Notify

The talent show judges will <u>notify</u> the winner on Friday. The contestants are nervously waiting to be informed of who won the contest.

(Cat video) We need to <u>notify</u> the homeowner that our project is going to take longer than we expected. We will be letting them know this as soon as we can.

Definition:_____

_____

4. Novice

Liam was a <u>novice</u> in the field of carpentry. Since he was a beginner, he still had much to learn.

(Cat video) I remember when I was a <u>novice</u> at guiding Santa's sled. It's never easy being new at a job, but I have learned so much since then.

Definition:_____

_____

5. Noxious

Drain cleaner is a <u>noxious</u> substance and is very harmful if a person drinks it.

(Cat video) As firefighters, we wear protective gear to keep us safe from <u>noxious</u> fumes. The smoke that we encounter is harmful, and we need to keep our lungs safe.

Definition:_____

_____

6. Obligation

The new employees have an <u>obligation</u> to attend employee training. The training sessions are a commitment they must fulfill.

(Cat video) In working on the construction site, we must meet the <u>obligations</u> set forth by the local community. We are required by law to have the proper permits and follow state rules.

Definition:_____

_____

7. Oblivious

Marjorie walked down the street in the pouring rain and seemed <u>oblivious</u> to the fact that it was raining. It was as if she did not even realize it.

(Cat video) When some people are talking on the phone, they are so <u>oblivious</u> to what is going on around them. It's as if they are so preoccupied, they don't even notice.

Definition:_____

_____

8. Obsequious

The <u>obsequious</u> student was constantly helping his professor. He was excessively willing to help because he wanted a good grade in the class.

(Cat video) Being a fairy godparent is an <u>obsequious</u> position. I need to be servile and overly willing to help anyone at any moment.

Definition:_____

_____

9. Obsess

The teenage girl became <u>obsessed</u> with her weight. She constantly weighed herself, and all she could talk about was how much she weighed.

(Cat video) As a cat, I must admit I <u>obsess</u> over chasing birds. It's something I can't seem to get enough of, and it just haunts my mind.

Definition:_____

_____

10. Obtuse

Jerry saw Georgia as <u>obtuse</u> since she was slow to understand his joke.

(Cat video) It isn't easy being as intelligent as I am. Often when I speak to other cats, I find they're somewhat <u>obtuse</u>. They're a little dull, and they're slow to understand what I am talking about.

Definition:_____

_____

List 3
Part 16

Useful ASVAB Vocabulary Words

Omit to Passive

1. Omit

Tony will <u>omit</u> a few items from the grocery list. He will leave out the items he does not really need.

(Cat video) When I tell scary stories, I make sure I don't <u>omit</u> a single detail. If I leave out any part, the story wouldn't be nearly as scary.

Definition:_____

_____

2. Omnipotent

When people have faith in God, they believe He is <u>omnipotent</u> or all-powerful.

(Cat video) As an angel, I believe that God is <u>omnipotent</u>. That means He is all-powerful.

Definition:_____

_____

3. Onus

When someone makes an accusation against another person, the <u>onus</u> of proof is on the accuser. The burden of proving it to be true lies upon the person making the accusation.

(Cat video) The <u>onus</u> is on me to get all this laundry folded. Laundry is such a burden and a heavy responsibility for me.

Definition:_____

_____

4. Optimum

It is a challenge to find an avocado at <u>optimum</u> ripeness. There is a short amount of time that the avocado is in the most favorable condition to be eaten.

(Cat video) In order to prepare for a fight, you must train hard if you want the <u>optimum</u> results. And I do because I always aim for the most favorable outcome.

Definition:_____

_____

5. Origin

Many people argue over the <u>origin</u> of the world. While some believe the beginning started with a big bang, others believe that God set the world in motion.

(Cat video) The <u>origin</u> of the Pilgrims was England. That place was the beginning of their journey. It was the source from which they came.

Definition:_____

_____

6. Ostentatious

The house that won the Christmas light show had an <u>ostentatious</u> display, a very showy and flashy presentation.

(Cat video) As America's most eligible feline bachelor, I have an engagement ring ready for the moment when I meet the girl of my dreams. I wonder if it is a little too <u>ostentatious,</u> but I'm a flashy kind of guy. So, I guess she will just have to accept a showy kind of ring because that is who she is going to be with.

Definition:_____

_____

7. Ostracize

Because of her physical disability, Regina was <u>ostracized</u> from the group. She was upset that people excluded her from their group.

(Cat video) I'm very sad when my peers <u>ostracize</u> me. It isn't easy to be excluded from a group when all I want to do is belong.

Definition:_____

_____

8. Pacify

Holding the teddy bear will <u>pacify</u> the baby. His toys help to soothe him and calm him down.

(Cat video) My stuffed animal helps to <u>pacify</u> me. It soothes me when I get stressed out.

Definition:_____

_____

9. Paradox

The young man made a statement that was a <u>paradox</u>. He said, "I know one thing, that I know nothing." His statement seemed like a contradiction but had truth in it.

(Cat video) Whenever I hear a <u>paradox,</u> it always makes me think deeply because contradictory statements are so very interesting.

Definition:_____

_____

10. Passive

The <u>passive</u> child was picked on by a bully and never answered him back.

(Cat video) Snuggles has always been much more <u>passive</u> than I am. He doesn't stand up for himself, and he is very meek.

Definition:_____

_____

List 3
Part 17

Useful ASVAB Vocabulary Words

Peculiar to Predicament

1. Peculiar

Ricky thought it was <u>peculiar</u> that his coworker talked to himself. This behavior seemed odd to him.

(Cat video) I have been told this wig looks <u>peculiar</u> on me. People say its odd, out of the ordinary. I guess they're right.

Definition:_____

_____

2. Persist

When the young man broke his wrist, he decided to <u>persist</u> in his goal of becoming a Marine. He refused to give up.

(Cat video) To reach your goals in life, it is important to <u>persist</u>, even if you come across opposition.

Definition:_____

_____

3. Petulance

Whenever Thomas did not get what he wanted, he showed the <u>petulance</u> of a toddler, in throwing a tantrum.

(Cat video) After the other team lost the game, one of the players showed his <u>petulance</u> by fighting with the referee. He threw a childlike tantrum instead of accepting the loss.

Definition:_____

_____

4. Placid

The vacation spot was very placid. Its calmness was very soothing to the vacation goers.

(Cat video) When I meditate, I feel so placid. It is so soothing to feel this calm and peaceful.

Definition:_____

_____

5. Plethora

The candy store had a plethora of sweets from which to choose. There was such an overabundance of candy there.

(Cat video) When we celebrated Thanksgiving we had a plethora of food. It was wonderful to have such an oversupply.

Definition:_____

_____

6. Poignant

The movie about the child suffering from cancer was a poignant film that brought tears to many eyes.

(Cat video) I really enjoyed hearing the poignant speech about Fluffy. It was really moving, and it touched my emotions deeply.

Definition:_____

_____

7. Pragmatic

Becky was proud to consider herself pragmatic since she saw value in being practical in life.

(Cat video) When a problem comes up, I come up with a pragmatic solution because I am always practical.

Definition:_____

_____

8. Precarious

Window washing without being secured with a harness would leave a person in a precarious situation. It is far too risky to do this without proper safety precautions.

(Cat video) When people refuse to leave their home in a hurricane evacuation, they are left in a precarious situation. They are left in an insecure and unstable environment.

Definition:_____

_____

9. Predator

Owls are predators of mice. They kill and eat small rodents.

(Cat video) The lion is a predator. It preys, destroys, and devours many animals that live in the jungle.

Definition:_____

_____

10. Predicament

When the child broke the window with a baseball and the principal saw it happen, the child was in quite a predicament. He knew that this was a truly unpleasant situation.

(Cat video) When I find myself in a predicament, and I realize this troublesome situation seems to have no escape, I just take a nap.

Definition:_____

_____

List 3
Part 18

Useful ASVAB Vocabulary Words

Prejudiced to Prolong

1. Prejudiced

Being <u>prejudiced</u> against others involves having an unfair dislike of them without even knowing them.

(Cat video) Our world has no time for people who are <u>prejudiced</u>. It is not right to judge something in advance without having enough evidence. We don't need to be biased. Everyone should be fair.

Definition:_____

_____

2. Premature

The baby was 6 weeks <u>premature</u>. She was born much earlier than expected.

(Cat video) My brothers and I were <u>premature</u> kittens. We were born before we were supposed to be, and we were so tiny at birth.

Definition:_____

_____

3. Primary

The school's <u>primary</u> focus is to provide a safe learning environment for children. This is the first goal of the school.

(Cat video) My <u>primary</u> goal is to have an amazing nap. This is my first and most important goal for today.

Definition:_____

_____

4. Principal

Sean got the role as the <u>principal</u> actor in the play, and he was very excited about having the lead role.

(Cat video) The <u>principal</u> foods in my diet consist of wet cat food and dry cat food. These are the main or most important part of my diet. The other stuff is the food I steal off my owner's plate when she's not looking.

Definition:_____

_____

5. Proclaim

The politician decided to <u>proclaim</u> that he had won the election. His announcement was heard on the radio.

(Cat video) When we win the battle, we will <u>proclaim</u> our victory. We will announce it loudly and publicly.

Definition:_____

_____

6. Procrastinate

There is no reason to <u>procrastinate</u> in life. Why put off until tomorrow, what you can do today?

(Cat video) When you want to get in shape, it's never a good idea to <u>procrastinate</u>. Why would you delay doing something and putting it off without reason? Get started today.

Definition:_____

_____

7. Profound

The philosophy professor liked to discuss <u>profound</u> topics, which caused his students to think deeply.

(Cat video) I like to study <u>profound</u> topics that make me reflect with much thought. I like thinking about intense things.

Definition:_____

_____

8. Profusely

Derek thanked his girlfriend <u>profusely</u> for all she had done for him. He thanked her abundantly, over and over again.

(Cat video) Anyone who takes my aerobics class sweats <u>profusely</u>. You too can sweat excessively if you sign up for my class.

Definition:_____

_____

9. Prohibit

Many schools <u>prohibit</u> the use of cell phones. They prevent students from using their phones so they will not be distracted in school.

(Cat video) At the scene of the fire, we needed to <u>prohibit</u> people from returning into the burning building. We prevented them from going in to keep them safe.

Definition:_____

_____

10. Prolong

Casey was having such a good time on his vacation that he decided to <u>prolong</u> his trip. He figured he might as well stay longer since he was enjoying his stay so much.

(Cat video) I'm so tired I might have to <u>prolong</u> my nap. I need to make it even longer.

Definition:_____

_____

List 3
Part 19

Useful ASVAB Vocabulary Words

Promote to Rancor

1. Promote

Jessie's hard work has paid off since his boss plans to promote him to a better paying position.

(Cat video) The way that you can promote from one rank to the next in the military requires lots of hard work. Because of this hard work, you can advance to a higher position.

Definition:_____

_____

2. Prompt

The taxi driver was prompt. He knew how important it was to be on time.

(Cat video) Life in the military requires you to be prompt. That means be on time. No excuses!

Definition:_____

_____

3. Protest

The animal rights supporters protested outside the company that takes part in animal testing. The protest showed their disapproval of those practices.

(Cat video) My animal friends and I are planning a protest against animal abuse. We plan to speak out against and to complain about this issue.

Definition:_____

_____

4. Proximity

Never leave your food in close <u>proximity</u> to your pet, if your pet likes to eat all the food they can reach.

(Cat video) Many people are concerned about my <u>proximity</u> to this iron, but I can assure you don't worry that I am so close I am to it. It isn't plugged in!

Definition:_____

_____

5. Prudent

It is <u>prudent</u> to save money since it is a wise idea to plan for the future.

(Cat video) When preparing for battle, it is important to make <u>prudent</u> decisions. Being wise and careful is necessary.

Definition:_____

_____

6. Punctuality

The bus driver was known for her <u>punctuality</u>. No matter what, she was always on time.

(Cat video) In basic training and boot camp, you will learn the importance of <u>punctuality</u>. So that when we say you need to be on time, you better be on time.

Definition:_____

_____

7. Quarrel

The young couple had their first <u>quarrel</u>, and they were very upset by this fight.

(Cat video) Snuggles and I had a bit of a <u>quarrel</u>. It's okay to argue or disagree about something, as long as you make up in the end.

Definition:_____

_____

169

8. Quench

When Joshua wanted to put out the campfire, he poured water on it to <u>quench</u> it.

(Cat video) As a firefighter, my job is to <u>quench</u> fires. I work very hard to put out all the fires I come across.

Definition:_____

_____

9. Query

During the interview, the reporter will <u>query</u> the celebrity about his new movie. She has many questions to ask him.

(Cat video) I often <u>query</u> my students about the material I just taught. What better way to assess their knowledge than to question them about it?

Definition:_____

_____

10. Rancor

After her friend betrayed her, Barbara had much <u>rancor</u> toward her. She could not get over the bitterness or anger she felt for her.

(Cat video) Pirates are filled with <u>rancor</u>. That's right. We are filled with ill will, malice, and anger against our enemies.

Definition:_____

_____

List 3
Part 20

Useful ASVAB Vocabulary Words

Random to Repress

1. Random

Winning the lottery happens by <u>random</u>. There is no way to plan to win since it happens by chance.

(Cat video) The winning lottery numbers are picked at <u>random</u>. They are chosen in an unplanned way without any order or pattern.

Definition:_____

_____

2. Recede

As men get older, many notice that their hairline will <u>recede</u>. It moves backward as balding approaches.

(Cat video) After the flood settles down, the water will <u>recede</u>. When it does go back, the waterline will be back to its normal position.

Definition:_____

_____

3. Recur

The medical treatments will reduce the chance that the cancer will <u>recur</u>. Even with treatments, the cancer could still come back.

(Cat video) I have a dream that always seems to <u>recur</u>. It's always me chasing a bird. I don't know why but this dream happens again and again and again.

Definition:_____

_____

4. Redundant

The term "exact same" is a <u>redundant</u> expression since it exceeds what is needed. "Exact" and "same" mean the same thing.

(Cat video) Some people use <u>redundant</u> expressions in their speech. For example, when someone says maybe I will, maybe I won't. That's excessively wordy. They could have just said maybe. It means the same thing without repeating themselves.

Definition:_____

_____

5. Refrain

In order to lose weight, Nicky must <u>refrain</u> from eating sweets. Keeping himself from eating sweets will help with his weight loss.

(Cat video) I have been told by my owner to <u>refrain</u> from eating the birds in the backyard. Can you imagine someone trying to keep me from eating birds? Sheesh!

Definition:_____

_____

6. Regimen

Many fitness experts follow a certain <u>regimen</u> to improve their health.

(Cat video) I follow a strict beauty <u>regimen</u>. I make sure I have a routine in place to keep my appearance looking youthful. It's not easy being an Internet sensation.

Definition:_____

_____

7. Reiterate

Mothers often <u>reiterate</u> what they want their children to do because they know that children need to be told things repeatedly at times.

(Cat video) An important part of being a professor is to make sure you <u>reiterate</u> your point. As a professor, I always make sure that I repeat myself so people will remember the lesson.

Definition:_____

_____

Julie A. Hyers © 2020

8. Relevant

During the court case, the judge reminded the lawyer to ask only <u>relevant</u> questions since he needed to remain focused on the important details.

(Cat video) When writing a research paper, focus on <u>relevant</u> topics. Concern yourself with the matter at hand, and focus on what is important.

Definition:_____

_____

9. Reluctant

The toddler was <u>reluctant</u> to put his coat on. He was unwilling to wear his coat even though it was freezing outside.

(Cat video) As pirates, we are often <u>reluctant</u> to do what anyone tells us to do because we are often opposing or unwilling to cooperate with anyone.

Definition:_____

_____

10. Repress

It is not good to <u>repress</u> feelings because when people hold back their emotions, they can suffer even more deeply.

(Cat video) It is not good to <u>repress</u> your feelings. Holding back feelings can cause even more problems. So let them all out! Can someone pass me the tissues?

Definition:_____

_____

List 3
Part 21

Useful ASVAB Vocabulary Words

Requisite to Ruminate

1. Requisite

Passing the ASVAB is a <u>requisite</u> for joining the military. It is a required or necessary part of enlisting.

(Cat video) Building permits are a <u>requisite</u> part in any construction job. They are required and necessary.

Definition:_____

_____

2. Resent

Candace <u>resented</u> her younger brother since she had to do all the chores while he did none. She felt bitterness over this.

(Cat video) As a superhero, I <u>resent</u> the villains. The bad guys really annoy me.

Definition:_____

_____

3. Reserve

Lynette will call the restaurant to <u>reserve</u> a table for her party. They will save the table for her and her friends.

(Cat video) When I grant wishes, I remind people to <u>reserve</u> some of the wishes for later on. It is good to save a wish for a later time.

Definition:_____

_____

4. Restrict

As part of Emily's diet, she works to <u>restrict</u> the number of calories she eats each day. By limiting her calories, she hopes to lose weight.

(Cat video) This outfit <u>restricts</u> my movement. It confines me and limits how much I can move.

Definition:_____

_____

5. Resume

After her operation, Virginia stopped exercising. She plans to <u>resume</u> her exercise 8 weeks after the surgery.

(Cat video) We stop working on the construction site when the weather is stormy, and we <u>resume</u> when the weather improves. We begin again after the interruption.

Definition:_____

_____

6. Retain

The child <u>retained</u> her balance after spinning around in a circle numerous times. It was not easy to keep her balance, but she did.

(Cat video) I like to wear a scarf in the winter months. It helps me to <u>retain</u> my body heat. It is really important to keep whatever heat you have in these cold days.

Definition:_____

_____

7. Retroactive

The teachers got a <u>retroactive</u> raise dating back to the beginning of the school year. Their raise will take effect for the past several months.

(Cat video) I am getting a raise at work. I hear the raise will be <u>retroactive</u> so it will go back to the beginning of the year.

Definition:_____

_____

8. Revive

The paramedic needed to <u>revive</u> the child who had drowned and was not breathing and did not have a pulse.

(Cat video) When I arrived at the fire, there was a kitten that I needed to <u>revive</u>. He was not breathing and he did not have a pulse. After I brought him back to life, he is doing fine. He was checked out in the hospital and returned to his mother and his litter.

Definition:_____

_____

9. Rue

The burglar regrets burglarizing the house and <u>rues</u> the day that he committed this crime.

(Cat video) We arrived at the scene of a fire that had been set on purpose. This fire destroyed three homes. It's a very upsetting thing to see, but we know that the day will come when the one who set the fire will <u>rue</u> the day that he did this. It might not be today, but he will be sorry, and he will regret what he did.

Definition:_____

_____

10. Ruminate

Marcia had two job offers and realized she had to <u>ruminate</u> over which job to choose. This would be something that would require great thought.

(Cat video) I <u>ruminate</u> over the meaning of life. I think deeply about this.

Definition:_____

_____

List 3
Part 22

Useful ASVAB Vocabulary Words

Salient to Squalid

1. Salient

The young boy's <u>salient</u> feature was his bright red hair. It was the first thing anyone would notice about him.

(Cat video) A <u>salient</u> feature of a cat is its whiskers. You cannot look at my face without noticing my obvious whiskers.

Definition:_____

_____

2. Satiate

The feast will <u>satiate</u> the hunger of the guests. There is more than enough for everyone.

(Cat video) At holiday dinners, I <u>satiate</u> myself with food. I fill myself to capacity.

Definition:_____

_____

3. Scant

The homeless man was so hungry because he only ate a <u>scant</u> amount of food today.

(Cat video) As kittens, before we were adopted, we had a <u>scant</u> amount of food. It was a very inadequate amount, and we were so hungry.

Definition:_____

_____

4. Scorn

Aaliyah looked on Michelle with <u>scorn</u> since she stole her boyfriend. Aaliyah felt contempt for her and viewed her as worthless.

(Cat video) I treat anyone who abuses animals with <u>scorn</u>. I have total disrespect for them.

Definition:_____

_____

5. Scrupulous

Herbert is a <u>scrupulous</u> accountant since he is very thorough with his work and pays close attention to detail.

(Cat video) I am proud of the fact that I am <u>scrupulous</u>. I make a conscious effort to be honest and upright.

Definition:_____

_____

6. Secure

Always keep your belongings in a <u>secure</u> place to make sure they are safe.

(Cat video) After removing people from the burning building, I needed to place them in a <u>secure</u> area, that way I knew they were safe.

Definition:_____

_____

7. Sentimental

When Janice sees photographs from her childhood, she becomes <u>sentimental</u>. It brings out her sensitive feelings with a hint of sadness.

(Cat video) I'm a <u>sentimental</u> sort of fellow. I am influenced by my emotion more than reason or thought. My heart rules me, far more than my head.

Definition:_____

_____

8. Slate

The personal trainer will <u>slate</u> Audra into her schedule for next week. He will arrange for their coaching session to happen.

(Cat video) I hear you are having a party that needs to be catered. We need to speak so I can I <u>slate</u> you into my schedule. Let me put you on my list.

Definition:_____

_____

9. Spiteful

The <u>spiteful</u> old woman held onto her anger for the one who did her wrong and plotted cruel revenge.

(Cat video) Pirates are known for our <u>spiteful</u> nature. We are mean, unkind and hurtful.

Definition:_____

_____

10. Squalid

The homeless children were living in <u>squalid</u> conditions. Their conditions were unclean and wretched.

(Cat video) We were living in <u>squalid</u> conditions before we were rescued. We were living in a flooded out area that was infested with ticks. We lived in a wretched, miserable and filthy environment at the time.

Definition:_____

_____

179

List 3
Part 23

Useful ASVAB Vocabulary Words

Stealthy to Superior

1. Stealthy

To be a good spy, one has to be <u>stealthy</u>, making sure you are not seen or heard.

(Cat video) As a ninja, I am very <u>stealthy</u>. I need to be so I can sneak up on people and plan my attack.

Definition:_____

_____

2. Strident

The whistle made a <u>strident</u> sound that was very shrill and harsh sounding.

(Cat video) Certain small dogs have such <u>strident</u> barks. There's another reason to adopt a cat. No harsh sounding barks will ever come from a cat!

Definition:_____

_____

3. Subordinate

In the military, the privates are <u>subordinate</u> to the sergeants and must honor their requests since the privates are in a lower rank.

(Cat video) When you join the military, remember you enter as a <u>subordinate</u>. You are in a lower rank, and you must answer to the higher authorities.

Definition:_____

_____

4. Substantial

After working in the business world for many years, Arthur had accumulated a <u>substantial</u> amount of wealth. He was known for his considerable wealth.

(Cat video) I need to prepare a <u>substantial</u> amount of food for the party I am catering because this party is significantly large.

Definition:_____

_____

5. Subtle

Leslie gave her husband a <u>subtle</u> hint of what she wanted for her birthday. She tried not to be too obvious when she pointed out the bracelet in the catalog.

(Cat video) I like to give <u>subtle</u> hints to my owner when I am hungry. I walk over to the food bowl; and I look at it, and I look at her. This is a simple method. Not very easily noticed. I try to take this mild approach to getting what I need.

Definition:_____

_____

6. Succinct

The instructor gave <u>succinct</u> directions, making sure he was clear and brief in his explanation.

(Cat video) When you need to make a point, it is best to be <u>succinct</u>. Keep it simple and to the point.

Definition:_____

_____

7. Sufficient

Wanda has a <u>sufficient</u> amount of food to feed her family for tonight. She has enough to last for today.

(Cat video) On Thanksgiving, we had a <u>sufficient</u> amount of food. There was enough for everyone.

Definition:_____

_____

8. Superficial

Stacy fell off her bicycle and suffered from <u>superficial</u> wounds. Her wounds were not deep and were only surface wounds.

(Cat video) Some people call me <u>superficial</u>. They say I am concerned with the surface only, and I am shallow just because I put so much time and effort into my appearance.

Definition:_____

_____

9. Superfluous

The banquet has a <u>superfluous</u> amount of food. There was an excessive amount of food available.

(Cat video) At Thanksgiving dinner, there is a <u>superfluous</u> amount of food, much more than what is needed.

Definition:_____

_____

10. Superior

Link is <u>superior</u> to Mark in his math ability. Math was always Link's strongest subject.

(Cat video) The lion is known as the <u>superior</u> animal in the jungle. It is obvious that he is above the others. Why else would he be known as the king of the jungle?

Definition:_____

_____

<u>**List 3**</u>
<u>**Part 24**</u>

<u>**Useful ASVAB Vocabulary Words**</u>

Supplement to Vacant

1. Supplement

Maggie will <u>supplement</u> her income by getting a second job. Her second job will add to her regular income.

(Cat video) I started teaching an aerobics class to <u>supplement</u> my income. My salary from this class will add to my weekly pay.

Definition:_____

_____

2. Surfeit

Sophie had a <u>surfeit</u> of candy after trick or treating on Halloween. It was more candy than she could even eat.

(Cat video) When Thanksgiving is over, I've had such a <u>surfeit</u> of turkey. I don't want to eat it for another year. Talk about an excess of turkey!

Definition:_____

_____

3. Suspend

The bus strike will <u>suspend</u> bus service. No one knows how long the temporary stop in bus service will last.

(Cat video) As a school principal, sometimes I need to <u>suspend</u> students for misbehavior. When I do this, they are removed from school temporarily.

Definition:_____

_____

4. Sustain

Food and water are necessary to <u>sustain</u> us. Without food and water, we cannot maintain our existence.

(Cat video) If I am able to <u>sustain</u> a relationship with the right girl, I will propose to her. If the relationship is maintained and continued for a good amount of time, then I'll know she is the right one for me.

Definition:_____

_____

5. Sympathetic

Victor was <u>sympathetic</u> to his classmate who had lost his brother. He showed pity and sorrow for his experience.

(Cat video) An important part of being in the medical field is being <u>sympathetic</u> toward your patients. We must be understanding, caring, and concerned for our patients.

Definition:_____

_____

6. Tedious

The school nurse needed to perform the <u>tedious</u> task of checking each student's head for lice. This took a long time and was a slow and tiresome task.

(Cat video) Folding laundry can be such a <u>tedious</u> task. It can be so boring, long, or tiresome.

Definition:_____

_____

7. Terminate

The company will <u>terminate</u> Dolores's employment this month. She needs to find a new job after her current position ends.

(Cat video) People mistakenly think that graduation day is the day that your education will <u>terminate</u>. Education does not end. It is a lifelong process.

Definition:_____

_____

8. Transition

Sometimes it is difficult to know what to wear during the <u>transition</u> between spring and summer. Changing from one season to another brings some unpredictable temperature changes.

(Cat video) I like to wear a scarf when the weather starts to <u>transition</u> into winter. It's good to be prepared for the change that's coming.

Definition:_____

_____

9. Unethical

It was <u>unethical</u> for the man to pretend to be a doctor and to work on patients. This was morally wrong.

(Cat video) Pirates are known for being <u>unethical</u>. We are seen as having no moral principles, and we don't care what is right or wrong.

Definition:_____

_____

10. Vacant

The apartment had been <u>vacant</u> for a very long time. Since no one had rented it for a while, it had been empty for years.

(Cat video) A <u>vacant</u> building had burned down to the ground. We knew there were no injuries since this building was empty for a long time.

Definition:_____

_____

List 3
Part 25

Useful ASVAB Vocabulary Words

Vain to Wince

1. Vain

After many <u>vain</u> attempts at passing the exam, Leah realized she needed a tutor to help her to pass.

(Cat video) I keep making these <u>vain</u> attempts to fly like a butterfly. I don't know why I keep trying. I know my attempts are going to be unsuccessful and useless anyway.

Definition:_____

_____

2. Valid

There was <u>valid</u> evidence presented at the trial. It was legally acceptable evidence.

(Cat video) As a police officer when I pull people over who are driving, I need to make sure they have a <u>valid</u> driver's license. We need to make sure that based on the evidence this license is justifiable and real.

Definition:_____

_____

3. Vapid

The choice for best actress was a disappointment to Marilyn who viewed her as <u>vapid</u>. Marilyn saw that actress's performances as dull.

(Cat video) The new television show was so <u>vapid</u>. Ohhh, it just bored me to sleep.

Definition:_____

_____

4. Verify

The doorman asked for identification from the visitor so he could <u>verify</u> her identity. He needed to make sure she was who she said she was.

(Cat video) Upon listening to the witness's story, we will need to <u>verify</u> that. We will have to prove that story was true.

Definition:_____

_____

5. Vex

The troublesome child would <u>vex</u> his little sister. He enjoyed annoying her.

(Cat video) As a superhero, I know the villains often like to <u>vex</u> us superheroes. They work very hard to irritate and distress us, but they're not going to win.

Definition:_____

_____

6. Vigilant

The police told people to be <u>vigilant</u> after all the robberies in the neighborhood. They were told to be watchful and alert.

(Cat video) In order to reduce the chance of home robberies, we ask people to be <u>vigilant</u>. Be watchful. Stay on guard. Lock your doors, lock your windows, and watch out for your neighbors.

Definition:_____

_____

7. Vociferous

The children's birthday party was <u>vociferous</u>. With so many screaming children, it was a noisy place to be.

(Cat video) Pirates are <u>vociferous</u>. They are a noisy group.

Definition:_____

_____

8. Wince

When the bully punched the young boy in the eye, he <u>winced</u>. He shrank back in pain.

(Cat video) In my last fight, I watched my opponent <u>wince</u>. He shrank back from my blow and from the pain of my punch.

Definition:_____

_____

Useful ASVAB Vocabulary Words
<u>**Definitions**</u>

Part 1
1. Abandon - to give up completely, to desert, to leave
2. Abate - to become less
3. Abet - to help
4. Abolish - to do away with
5. Abort - to cut short
6. Abridge - to shorten
7. Abstain - to voluntarily do without, to refrain from
8. Acumen - sharpness of mind
9. Adequate - enough for what is required, sufficient
10. Adhere - to stick to a surface or to believe in and follow the practices of

Part 2
1. Adjourn - to close a meeting for a time
2. Adversary - opponent, foe, enemy
3. Advocate - one who speaks or writes in support of another
4. Agitate - to make someone nervous or troubled
5. Allude - to refer to indirectly, hint at
6. Aloof - cool and reserved, distant
7. Amicable - friendly, peaceful
8. Anomaly - abnormality
9. Assert - to state a fact or belief confidently or forcefully
10. Assess - to set a value on

Part 3
1. Attain - to gain
2. Atypical - abnormal
3. Baffle - to completely confuse
4. Banal - lacking in originality, obvious, and boring
5. Barren - fruitless, unproductive, infertile
6. Belie - to disguise or misrepresent
7. Bogus - not genuine, false
8. Boycott - to withdraw from relations with a country, organization, or person as a punishment or protest
9. Candid - very honest and open
10. Capricious - having sudden, impulsive thinking or actions

Part 4
1. Chaos - extreme confusion or disorder
2. Clandestine - secret or hidden
3. Coerce - to force
4. Cogent - convincing to the point

5. Coherent - logical and consistent, understandable
6. Collaborate -to work together
7. Colleague - a worker in the same profession
8. Comparable - able to be likened or compared to another
9. Compose - to make up or create
10. Compromise - an agreement that is reached by each side giving up something they wanted

Part 5
1. Concede - to give in, to surrender or yield
2. Concept - idea or thought
3. Concise - brief and to the point
4. Conduct - behavior
5. Confidential - meant to be kept secret
6. Conscientious - wishing to do what is right, especially to do one's work well
7. Consume - to use up
8. Contaminate - to make corrupt or pollute
9. Contempt - the feeling one has toward someone they view as worthless
10. Covert - hidden or disguised

Part 6
1. Creed - a statement of religious belief
2. Culpable - deserving blame
3. Dearth - scarcity or lack
4. Debilitate - to make weak
5. Deceive - to mislead or trick someone
6. Decimate - to destroy or kill a large part of
7. Decrepit - broken down or worn out by old age
8. Delete - to take out, to cross out
9. Demolish - to destroy

Part 7
1. Demote - to reduce to a lower rank
2. Deprive - to take away from forcibly
3. Detrimental - causing damage
4. Deviation - a departing from the accepted or normal standard
5. Diminish - to make or become smaller in size
6. Discard - to get rid of
7. Disclose - to reveal
8. Dismal - dark and gloomy
9. Diverse - different, varied
10. Docile - easy to discipline, submissive

Part 8
1. Dormant - inactive or sleeping state
2. Dubious - hesitating or doubting
3. Durable - something that lasts a long time, even with frequent use

4. Dwindle - to keep becoming smaller or less, to diminish or shrink
5. Eclectic - selected from various sources
6. Elusive - difficult to find, catch, or achieve
7. Empathy - the ability to share in another's emotions, thoughts, or feelings
8. Enable - to make able or possible
9. Enhance - to make greater or better
10. Enlightened - free from ignorance or prejudice

Part 9
1. Entitle - to give a title or a right or claim to something
2. Equivocal - having two or more meanings, purposely unclear
3. Evaluate - to find out the value of something
4. Evasive - seeking to avoid or escape by deceit or cleverness
5. Evoke - to call forth
6. Expel - to remove by force
7. Exploit - to use someone or something selfishly for profit
8. Extraneous - irrelevant or unrelated to the topic being dealt with
9. Facetious - joking especially at an inappropriate time
10. Fallacious - based on a mistaken belief

Part 10
1. Feasible - capable of being done, possible
2. Fickle - changeable, unstable, capricious
3. Forfeit - to lose or have taken away
4. Fortuitous - happening by chance, lucky
5. Fraudulent - trickery, deceit
6. Fundamental - forming a foundation or basis
7. Gracious - having or showing kindness, courtesy, or charm
8. Gregarious - sociable, enjoying company of others
9. Guile - sly, crafty, tricky
10. Harass - to make repeated attacks on someone

Part 11
1. Hectic - full of activity, very busy, fast
2. Hinder - to keep back, to stop
3. Illusion - a false idea or conception
4. Immune - protected from against something harmful
5. Impartial - fair, without bias
6. Impeccable - flawless, without error
7. Imply - to hint or suggest
8. Impressive - bringing about admiration of others
9. Inception - beginning or start
10. Indigenous - existing or growing naturally in a region or country

Part 12
1. Induct - to admit someone to a position or organization

2. Inferior - lower in order, status or rank

3. Initiate - to bring into practice or use

4. Innocuous - harmless

5. Innovation - the process of introducing new methods

6. Instinct - a natural or inborn tendency to behave a certain way

7. Intuition - the ability to acquire knowledge without proof or evidence

8. Irate - extremely angry

9. Itinerary - a detailed plan for a journey

10. Lament - to feel or express deep sorrow, to mourn

Part 13

1. Legible - able to be read

2. Leisurely - done without haste in a slow or unhurried manner

3. Lethargic - drowsy, sluggish

4. Lithe - flexible

5. Loathe - to feel intense dislike or hatred

6. Lucid - clear, easily understood

7. Lucrative - producing wealth, profitable

8. Magnitude - greatness in size or extent

9. Malleable - able to be hammered or changed into different shapes without breaking

10. Mediocre - ordinary, average

Part 14

1. Mend - to repair or make better

2. Meritorious - deserving reward or praise

3. Minute - very small

4. Misnomer - a wrong name

5. Mitigate - to make less severe

6. Morose - gloomy

7. Motivation - the reason one has for acting or behaving in a certain way

8. Mundane - worldly, commonplace, ordinary

9. Naïve - gullible, quick to believe what one is told

10. Nascent - beginning to form or develop

Part 15

1. Neglectful - failing to give proper care to something or someone; careless, inattentive

2. Nonchalant - casually calm or relaxed

3. Notify - to inform

4. Novice - a beginner

5. Noxious - harmful

6. Obligation - a duty or commitment

7. Oblivious - not aware of or concerned about what is happening around oneself

8. Obsequious - having an excessive willingness to serve others

9. Obsess - to haunt or trouble the mind

10. Obtuse - slow to understand

Part 16

1. Omit - to leave out
2. Omnipotent - having unlimited power or authority, all-powerful
3. Onus - burden
4. Optimum - best or most favorable condition
5. Origin - beginning
6. Ostentatious - showy display
7. Ostracize - to exclude someone from a group
8. Pacify - to soothe, calm
9. Paradox - a statement that seems contradictory but is true
10. Passive - accepting or allowing what happens or what others do without active response

Part 17
1. Peculiar - odd, strange
2. Persist - to refuse to give up
3. Petulance - the quality of being easily annoyed by minor things, like a bad-tempered child
4. Placid - calm, quiet
5. Plethora - overabundance, excess
6. Poignant - emotionally moving
7. Pragmatic - practical
8. Precarious - risky
9. Predator - an animal that lives by killing and eating other animals or a person who seeks to use others to control them
10. Predicament - a difficult, unpleasant or embarrassing situation

Part 18
1. Prejudiced - having an unfair dislike of a person or group beforehand
2. Premature - arriving before the proper or usual time, too early
3. Primary - first in order
4. Principal - first in rank or importance
5. Proclaim - to announce officially
6. Procrastinate - to put off doing until later, delay
7. Profound - having great knowledge or insight
8. Profusely - abundantly, in large amounts
9. Prohibit - to forbid or prevent
10. Prolong - to lengthen in time or space

Part 19
1. Promote - to raise to a higher position or rank
2. Prompt - on time
3. Protest - to express disapproval
4. Proximity - nearness
5. Prudent - acting wisely showing care and thought for the future
6. Punctuality - being on time or prompt
7. Quarrel - a dispute or a fight
8. Quench - to put out a fire, to satisfy one's thirst
9. Query - question, inquiry

10. Rancor - bitterness or resentfulness

Part 20
1. Random - purposeless, happening by chance
2. Recede - to move or go backward
3. Recur - to happen repeatedly
4. Redundant - exceeding what is needed
5. Refrain - to hold back, to keep oneself from doing something
6. Regimen - a system to improve one's health
7. Reiterate - to say or do again repeatedly
8. Relevant - relating to the matter at hand, important
9. Reluctant - unwilling
10. Repress - to hold back, restrain

Part 21
1. Requisite - required or necessary
2. Resent - to feel sorrow or show displeasure or hurt, bitterness
3. Reserve - to save for later
4. Restrict - to keep within limits
5. Resume - to continue after interruption
6. Retain - to continue to have or keep possession of
7. Retroactive - having an effect on things that are already past
8. Revive - to bring back to life
9. Rue - to feel regret or be sorry for
10. Ruminate - to think deeply about something

Part 22
1. Salient - most noticeable or important
2. Satiate - to provide with more than enough, glut
3. Scant - inadequate, not enough
4. Scorn - the feeling or belief that someone or something is worthless
5. Scrupulous - diligent, thorough, and extremely attentive to details
6. Secure - free from danger, safe
7. Sentimental - showing feelings of tenderness, sadness, or remembrance of the past
8. Slate - to arrange for something to happen
9. Spiteful - cruel, mean, vengeful
10. Squalid - unclean or wretched

Part 23
1. Stealthy - behaving in a cautious way so not to be seen or heard
2. Strident - harsh-sounding, shrill
3. Subordinate - below another in rank or importance
4. Substantial - of considerable importance, size, or worth
5. Subtle - not obvious
6. Succinct - clear and brief
7. Sufficient - as much as is needed, enough

8. Superficial - existing or occurring on the surface
9. Superfluous - excessive or unnecessary
10. Superior - higher in order, rank, etc.

Part 24
1. Supplement - something added to make up for lack
2. Surfeit - an excessive amount of something, too much
3. Suspend - to stop temporarily
4. Sustain - to keep in existence, to maintain
5. Sympathetic - feeling, showing, or expressing pity or sorrow for someone else's misfortunes
6. Tedious - long, slow, or tiresome
7. Terminate - to end or stop
8. Transition - passing from one condition or place to another, a change
9. Unethical - not morally correct, morally wrong
10. Vacant - empty

Part 25
1. Vain - producing no effect, useless; also means having a high opinion of one's appearance
2. Valid - reasonable or logical; legally or officially acceptable
3. Vapid - tasteless, dull
4. Verify - to prove to be true
5. Vex - to annoy
6. Vigilant - staying watchful and alert to danger
7. Vociferous - noisy
8. Wince - to shrink back in pain

Paragraph Comprehension Section

Paragraph Comprehension Tips

There are a number of tips that can help with the Paragraph Comprehension section of the ASVAB.

- Read the questions before reading the passage.

- Read every answer choice before selecting one. Even if you think you found the correct answer, read all of the answer choices before making your selection.

- Base your answers on the passage and not on your own opinions or background knowledge.

- Most of the time, an answer choice with the word "never" or "always" is not the correct one.

- Make sure you do not leave any answer blank on the test.

- Make educated guesses. Do not just randomly pick an answer choice.

- This is a timed test. Every second counts!

Remember, this is a multiple-choice test. The good news is that the answer is on the page before you. There are 4 choices before you, and you need to pick the correct one.

Let's examine how eliminating answer choices increases the odds of getting the correct answer.

There is a 25% chance of getting the right answer with a purely random guess when you have 4 answer choices.

If you can eliminate one choice, you are left with 3 choices, which raises your odds to a 33.33% chance of answering correctly by guessing.

If you can eliminate 2 choices, you have a 50% chance of answering correctly.

The bottom line is to read carefully and eliminate obvious wrong answers.

In reading passage questions with 4 choices, there is usually one answer that sounds almost ridiculous. Eliminate that one. Usually 2 answers sound somewhat reasonable, but your goal is to pick the best one. In each case, one answer is the best one.

There are different types of questions that can be asked in the Paragraph Comprehension section of the ASVAB.

Below are listed the most common types of questions that could be asked along with some tips on how to find the answers for each of these types.

Main Idea

Main Idea questions are very common. It asks you what the story was mostly about.

The main idea might be directly stated or implied or hinted at by the author. Main idea questions are less specific than some of the other questions. It asks about the general idea of the passage. It could be presented in different ways. The main idea might be directly stated or implied or hinted at by the author.

Some examples of main idea questions include:
What was the main idea of the story?
What was the story mostly about?
What would be a good title for the story?

In order to figure out the main idea of a story, focus on the first sentence of each paragraph and the last sentence of the story. Sometimes the entire passage must be read to find the main idea.

Detail

Detail questions are also common. These questions do not focus on the whole passage but instead on small pieces of information found within the story. Detail questions focus on specific information in the passage. Do not look for the main idea of the passage when answering a detail question.

Examples of detail questions focus on events or descriptions found in the passage.

Where was the missing ring found?
What was the occupation of the man with the raincoat?
Who was the one to solve the case?

In order to answer a detail question, skim through the passage looking for the detail for which the question is asking.
Do not fall for answers that are distracting you from the real answer.
Eliminate answers that were not stated in the passage.

Vocabulary

Vocabulary questions are found in this section. Answering a vocabulary question in this section provides an advantage that is not found in the Word Knowledge section. This section provides strong context clues for the vocabulary questions.

On the Word Knowledge section, some questions might say, "What does this word most nearly mean?" No context clue is given to help you. Vocabulary questions on the Paragraph Comprehension section can be a bit easier because the context clues help to determine the meaning of the word.

Examples of vocabulary questions include:

What does the word "frazzled" most nearly mean?
What did the driver mean when he said, "he felt he was under his boss's thumb"?

Make sure you read the words and sentences around the vocabulary word or the expression in question. The clues around the word will help you to figure out the answer.

Sometimes there will be an answer choice that sounds like or rhymes with the vocabulary word being asked about. This is usually a trap.

For example: What does *auspicious* mean?
Do NOT pick "suspicious" as an answer choice. Rhyming words tend to be trap answers.

Make sure you read the meaning of the word in the context of the story. Many words in English have multiple meanings.
An example is the word "pedestrian". Pedestrian means a person who walks. It also means commonplace or ordinary.
Always read the passage to see the meaning that is being presented.

Sequence

Sequence questions will refer to the order of events in the story. Pay attention to words relating to sequence: first, then, next, after that, finally, at last, before, after, etc.
To answer sequence questions, read with attention to order of events.

Examples of sequence questions include:

What was the last ingredient that needed to be added to Grandma's apple pie recipe?
What did the farmer do before he plowed the field?

Inference

Inference questions call for the reader to read between the lines. The answer will not be directly stated in the passage, but enough information will be given to help the reader make an educated conclusion.
In answering inference questions, base the answer on the passage and not on your personal opinion or background knowledge.

Examples of inference questions are:

Due to the new mayor's strong focus on education, what will he most likely seek to achieve in his first term?
What would be a possible result of speeding up the assembly line at the car factory?

To answer inference questions, do not look for the answer to be directly stated in the text. Read the passage and think beyond what is written there. It is where you put the pieces of a puzzle together to come to a conclusion based on presented facts.

Cause and Effect

Cause and Effect questions seek to examine the cause and the result of certain actions and events. The passage could tell why something happened and the results.

Examples of cause and effect questions are:

What happened as a result of the firing of the beloved teacher?
What caused the protests to take place?

Certain words indicate cause and effect within a passage. There are key words to look for in order to find the answers to cause and effect questions: as a result, because, since, as a consequence, etc.

Author's Tone

Author's Tone is a question that asks you to read into how the author sounds when he wrote the passage. Is he being funny? Sarcastic? Angry? Factual?
Examine the words he uses to see how he feels.
Author's Tone is not something directly stated in the passage. You must pick up on how the author sounds. It could also be called his attitude in the passage.

Examples of Author's Tone questions are:

What is the author's tone in the passage?
What is the author's attitude toward the congressional candidate?

In answering an Author's Tone question, think about whether the author comes across in a positive or negative way regarding the topic at hand. The topic could also be presented very factually in a scientific or historical way, neither positively nor negatively.

Author's Purpose

Author's Purpose is different from author's tone. Some people confuse the two.
The author's purpose is why the passage was written.

I like to remember it as PIE.
Three type of author's purpose are:
P - Persuade
I - Inform
E - Entertain

If the author is trying to persuade you, he is trying to convince you to vote for a certain candidate, to buy a certain car, to influence your choice of movies, etc.

If the author is trying to inform you, his passage is a factual one, possibly a scientific or historical piece.

If the author is trying to entertain you, his passage could be funny, sarcastic, or ironic.

Examples of Author's Purpose questions are:

Why did the author write this piece?
What message is the author trying to convey about the new clothing line?

Passages in this packet were taken from www.gutenberg.org
The passages include different genres of literature including: nonfiction, fiction, editorials, folklore, myths, poetry, letters, and essays.

Passage 1

Domesticated Animals by Nathaniel Southgate Shaler

Swans

The swan, like the peacock, has been bred for ornament rather than for use. In fact, the bird has no other merit than its exceeding grace. We cannot believe that much pain was ever taken with this creature to break up the migratory instincts, which are common in the wild kindred species. We have to suppose that the bird in its pristine form was without the impulse to undertake distant journeys in the winter season, or that it abandoned ancient habits with no great difficulty. We obtain some light on this point by noting the fact that among the migratory species it not infrequently happens that, while the greater number of individuals undertake the annual journey, certain of them will remain on the ground where they were born. Those, which remain, would be more likely to mate with those, which were like-minded than with others that journeyed afar. In this way small local breeds might well be originated which would differ from their migratory kindred not only in the measure of the wandering instincts, but in the capacity for flight which their kindred preserve. There is some reason to believe that this process of selection naturally and somewhat frequently takes place. In certain cases it may lay the foundation of new species, or at least of distinct varieties; more commonly, however, the individuals, which have abandoned the migratory life are likely to perish from the severity of climate or the other unfavorable conditions that their mates avoid by their wanderings.

(Passage taken from gutenberg.org)

Main Idea

1. What does it mean that swans are bred for ornament and not use?

    A. Many ornaments have swans on them.
    B. Swans play an important role in completing tasks for mankind.
    C. Swans serve little other function than their beauty.
    D. Only beautiful swans reproduce.

Detail

2. What other bird does the author compare the swan to?

    A. a goose
    B. a duck
    C. a peacock
    D. a stork

Vocabulary

3. What does *perish* mean?

    A. cherish
    B. become sick
    C. fly away
    D. die

Author's Tone

4. What is the author's tone in this passage?

    A. The author takes on a humorous tone.
    B. The author takes on a critical tone
    C. The author takes on a grateful tone
    D. The author takes on anxious tone.

Passage 1

Domesticated Animals by Nathaniel Southgate Shaler
Swans

Answer Key

Answers and Explanations

Main Idea

1. What does it mean that swans are bred for ornament and not use?

C. Swans serve little other function than their beauty.

This is a main idea question and the answer is found in the first sentence of the passage.

"The swan, like the peacock, has been bred for ornament rather than for use. In fact, the bird has no other merit than its exceeding grace."

Detail

2. What other bird does the author compare the swan to?

C. a peacock

This is a detail question. Search through the passage for the place where the author compares a swan to another bird.

"The swan, like the peacock, has been bred for ornament rather than for use. In fact, the bird has no other merit than its exceeding grace."

Vocabulary

3. What does *perish* mean?

D. die

This is a vocabulary question. To figure out the meaning of the word "perish", read the sentences around the word to find context clues. The clues reveal that perish means to die.

"In certain cases it may lay the foundation of new species, or at least of distinct varieties; more commonly, however, the individuals, which have abandoned the migratory life are likely to perish from the severity of climate or the other unfavorable conditions that their mates avoid by their wanderings."

Author's Tone

4. What is the author's tone in this passage?

B. The author takes on a critical tone

The author criticized the idea that swans are bred for their beauty throughout the passage.

Passage 2

U.S. Department of Agriculture

Farmer's Bulletin 447
Bees
BEE BEHAVIOR

A colony of bees consists normally of one queen bee, the mother of the colony, and thousands of sexually undeveloped females called workers, which normally lay no eggs, but build the comb, gather the stores, keep the hive clean, feed the young, and do the other work of the hive. During part of the year there are also present some hundreds of males or drones (often removed or restricted in numbers by the bee keeper), whose only service is to mate with young queens. These three types are easily recognized, even by a novice. In nature the colony lives in a hollow tree or other cavity, but under manipulation thrives in the artificial hives provided. The combs, which form their abode, are composed of wax secreted by the workers. The hexagonal cells of the two vertical layers constituting each comb have interplaced ends on a common septum. In the cells of these combs are reared the developing bees, and honey and pollen for food are also stored here.

(Passage taken from gutenberg.org)

Main Idea

1. What is the main idea of this passage?

    A. The role of different members of a bee colony and the description of their home
    B. The way honey is made and how it is collected
    C. The dangers bees pose to some people
    D. The purpose of beeswax

Vocabulary

2. What does the word *novice* mean?

    A. insect
    B. someone who is new at something
    C. an expert
    D. doctor

Author's Tone

3. What is the author's tone in this piece?

    A. sarcastic
    B. funny
    C. factual
    D. angry

Author's Purpose

4. What was the author's purpose in writing this piece?

    A. To inform
    B. To entertain
    C. To persuade
    D. To contradict

Passage 2

Bee Behavior
Answer Key

Answers and Explanations

Main Idea

1. What is the main idea of this passage?

A. The role of different members of a bee colony and the description of their home

The main idea of the passage is found by reading this entire passage. In reading the passage, you realize that it is mostly about the roles of bees in the colony and their home.

Vocabulary

2. What does the word *novice* mean?

B. someone who is new at something

This is a vocabulary question. To answer a vocabulary question, look for the word "novice" and read the sentences around the word for context clues. The below sentence explains how certain types of bees can be easily recognized, even by a novice. The word "even" shows that a novice is someone who should not be expected to be able to recognize them but can. This proves that a novice must be a beginner.

"These three types are easily recognized, even by a novice."

Author's Tone

3. What is the author's tone in this piece?

C. Factual

The passage is an informational text of scientific facts, and the author's tone is factual.

Author's Purpose

4. What was the author's purpose in writing this piece?

A. To inform

The passage is an informational piece of scientific facts about bees, so the author's purpose is to inform.

Passage 3

Buccaneers and Pirates of Our Coasts By Frank R. Stockton

Chapter 1 The Bold Buccaneers

When I was a boy I strongly desired to be a pirate, and the reason for this was the absolute independence of that sort of life. Restrictions of all sorts had become onerous to me, and in my reading of the adventures of the bold sea-rovers of the main, I had unconsciously selected those portions of a pirate's life, which were attractive to me, and had totally disregarded all the rest.

In fact, I had a great desire to become what might be called a marine Robin Hood. I would take from the rich and give to the poor; I would run my long, low, black craft by the side of the merchantman, and when I had loaded my vessel with the rich stuffs and golden ingots which composed her cargo, I would sail away to some poor village, and make its inhabitants prosperous and happy for the rest of their lives by a judicious distribution of my booty.

I would always be as free as a sea-bird. My men would be devoted to me, and my word would be their law. I would decide for myself whether this or that proceeding would be proper, generous, and worthy of my unlimited power; when tired of sailing, I would retire to my island, —the position of which, in a beautiful semi-tropic ocean, would be known only to myself and to my crew, —and there I would pass happy days in the company of my books, my works of art, and all the various treasures I had taken from the mercenary vessels which I had overhauled.

Such was my notion of a pirate's life. I would kill nobody; the very sight of my black flag would be sufficient to put an end to all thought of resistance on the part of my victims, who would no more think of fighting me, than a fat bishop would have thought of lifting his hand against Robin Hood and his merry men; and I truly believe that I expected my conscience to have a great deal more to do in the way of approval of my actions, than it had found necessary in the course of my ordinary school-boy life.

I mention these early impressions because I have a notion that a great many people—and not only young people—have an idea of piracy not altogether different from that of my boyhood. They know that pirates are wicked men, that, in fact, they are sea-robbers or maritime murderers, but their bold and adventurous method of life, their bravery, daring, and the exciting character of their expeditions, give them something of the same charm and interest which belong to the robber knights of the middle ages. The one mounts his mailed steed and clanks his long sword against his iron stirrup, riding forth into the world with a feeling that he can do anything that pleases him, if he finds himself strong enough. The other springs into his rakish craft, spreads his sails to the wind, and dashes over the sparkling main with a feeling that he can do anything he pleases, provided he be strong enough.

(Passage taken from gutenberg.org)

Main Idea

1. What is the main idea of the story?

    A. Pirates have a positive impact on society.
    B. Too many people overlook the benefits that pirates bring to society.
    C. Pirates are the worst criminals of all.
    D. The young boy's desire to be a pirate was influenced by his false impression of what pirates really do.

Vocabulary

2. What does *judicious* mean?

    A. fair
    B. joyful
    C. suspicious
    D. illegal

Cause and Effect

3. What caused the boy to want to become a pirate?

    A. His love of the ocean
    B. He came from a family of pirates
    C. His desire to have the independence of pirate life
    D. His willingness to rob and steal

Sequence

4. Which topic was mentioned first?

    A. The boy's reason for wanting to be a pirate
    B. The boy's realization that pirates are criminals
    C. The boy's desire to be like Robin Hood
    D. The boy's willingness to ignore the bad aspects of pirates and focus only on the good

Passage 3

Buccaneers and Pirates of Our Coasts

Answer Key

Answers and Explanations

Main Idea

1. What is the main idea of the story?

 D.   The young boy's desire to be a pirate was influenced by his false impression of what pirates really do.

This is a main idea question. The answer to a main idea question is often found in the first sentence of the passage or the last sentence. However, it can be found anywhere. In this case, it is not found there.

"Restrictions of all sorts had become onerous to me, and in my reading of the adventures of the bold sea-rovers of the main, I had unconsciously selected those portions of a pirate's life which were attractive to me and had totally disregarded all the rest."

Vocabulary

2. What does *judicious* mean?

A. Fair

This question is a vocabulary question. To answer a vocabulary question, look for the word "judicious" and read the sentences around the word for context clues. The following sentence shows how the boy plans to steal from the rich to help the poor, which he views as judicious or fair.

"I would sail away to some poor village and make its inhabitants prosperous and happy for the rest of their lives by a judicious distribution of my booty."

Cause and Effect

3. What caused the boy to want to become a pirate?

C. His desire to have the independence of pirate life

This question is a cause and effect question. You need to find what caused the boy to want to become a pirate. The sentence has the word "reason" in it, which is a clue word in cause and effect type of questions.

"When I was a boy I strongly desired to be a pirate, and the reason for this was the absolute independence of that sort of life."

Sequence

4. Which topic was mentioned first?

A. The boy's reason for wanting to be a pirate

This is a sequence question that asks about what happened first. Go back to the passage and read the first topic that is mentioned.

"When I was a boy I strongly desired to be a pirate, and the reason for this was the absolute independence of that sort of life."

Passage 4

Editorial from the Hearst Newspapers by Arthur Brisbane

The Automobile Will Make Us More Human

One of the commonest and most disagreeable sights in a big city is that of a strong, brutal human being beating a weak and overworked horse because it refuses to do what it cannot do.

Brutality inflicted upon horses is atrocious. But the bad effect of such unkind treatment of animals on HUMAN CHARACTER is far more serious than the actual physical suffering inflicted.

The perfection of the automobile will do much to improve human beings by taking away from their control and from brutal coercion of submissive animals.

Everybody knows that the moral standard is raised immediately in a country when slavery is abolished.

In America we have abolished the slavery of human beings, but we still adhere to horse slavery, accompanied by all the worst forms of the old Negro slavery. The faithful slave may be beaten and driven to death. The driver MUST BE BRUTALIZED.

Every day, on every street, you may see stupid, muscular boys and men jerking with all their might on the tender mouths of poor horses, only too willing to do their best.

This brutal indifference to the sufferings of animals makes us brutal and indifferent in other directions.

With the advent of the automobile and the disappearance of horses from our cities, horse slavery will be abolished and men, compelled to use their brains in dealing with machinery, will soon become more nearly human than they are at present. The practical abolition of the street-car horse is one great step in advance.

The abolition of the truck horse, carriage horse, cab horse, soon to come, will complete the dream of those modern and highly deserving abolitionists, the automobile inventors and manufacturers.

(Passage taken from gutenberg.org)

Main Idea

1. What is the main idea of this story?

   A. Slavery is an evil of society.
   B. Abuse of horses by humans must be stopped.
   C. People need to assert control over horses.
   D. Horses can be vicious animals.

Inference

2. How does the author believe that automobiles will make people more human?

   A. People will stop treating horses as their slaves.
   B. Automobiles are a more advanced means of transportation.
   C. Driving cars will make traveling easier.
   D. People will spend less time traveling.

Author's Tone

3. What is the author's tone in this passage when it comes to human treatment of horses?

   A. admiration
   B. disgust
   C. approval
   D. cheerful

Author's Purpose

4. What is the author's purpose in this passage?

   A. To inform the reader about the latest inventions
   B. To discuss slave trade
   C. To draw attention to the abuse of horses by people
   D. To convince people to buy the latest inventions

Passage 4

Editorial from the Hearst Newspapers by Arthur Brisbane

The Automobile Will Make Us More Human

Answer Key

Answers and Explanations

Main Idea

1. What is the main idea of this story?

B. Abuse of horses by humans must be stopped.

This is a main idea question. The main idea is often found in the first or last sentence of the passage or in the first sentence of any of the paragraphs in the passage.

The first sentence of the passage hints at the main idea in this case.

"One of the commonest and most disagreeable sights in a big city is that of a strong, brutal human being beating a weak and overworked horse because it refuses to do what it cannot do."

The first sentence of the second paragraph also covers the main idea.

"Brutality inflicted upon horses is atrocious."

Inference

2. How does the author believe that automobiles will make people more human?

A. People will stop treating horses as their slaves.

This is an inference question where you need to come to a conclusion from the information given. The following sentence gives the needed information to come to a conclusion.

"The perfection of the automobile will do much to improve human beings by taking away from their control and from brutal coercion of submissive animals."

Author's Tone

3. What is the author's tone in this passage when it comes to human treatment of horses?

B. Disgust

This question asks about author's tone, which can be found throughout the passage.

"Brutality inflicted upon horses is atrocious. But the bad effect of such unkind treatment of animals on HUMAN CHARACTER is far more serious than the actual physical suffering inflicted."

Author's Purpose

4. What is the author's purpose in this passage?

C. To draw attention to the abuse of horses by people.

Throughout the passage, the author purpose can be found where it shows how the author wants to end the abuse of horses by people. The below line is one example.

"In America we have abolished the slavery of human beings, but we still adhere to horse slavery, accompanied by all the worst forms of the old Negro slavery. The faithful slave may be beaten and driven to death. The driver MUST BE BRUTALIZED."

Passage 5

Editorial Wild Oats
By Mark Twain

My First Literary Venture

I was a very smart child at the age of thirteen—an unusually smart child, I thought at the time. It was then that I did my first newspaper scribbling, and most unexpectedly to me it stirred up a fine sensation in the community. It did, indeed, and I was very proud of it, too. I was a printer's "devil," and a progressive and aspiring one. My uncle had me on his paper (the *Weekly Hannibal Journal*, two dollars a year, in advance—five hundred subscribers, and they paid in cord-wood, cabbages, and unmarketable turnips), and on a lucky summer's day he left town to be gone a week, and asked me if I thought I could edit one issue of the paper judiciously. Ah! didn't I want to try! Higgins was the editor on the rival paper. He had lately been jilted, and one night a friend found an open note on the poor fellow's bed, in which he stated that he could no longer endure life and had drowned himself in Bear Creek. The friend ran down there and discovered Higgins wading back to shore. He had concluded he wouldn't. The village was full of it for several days, but Higgins did not suspect it. I thought this was a fine opportunity. I wrote an elaborately wretched account of the whole matter, and then illustrated it with villainous cuts engraved on the bottoms of wooden type with a jack-knife—one of them a picture of Higgins wading out into the creek in his shirt, with a lantern, sounding the depth of the water with a walking-stick. I thought it was desperately funny and was densely unconscious that there was any moral obliquity about such a publication. Being satisfied with this effort, I looked around for other worlds to conquer, and it struck me that it would make good, interesting matter to charge the editor of a neighboring country paper with a piece of gratuitous rascality and "see him squirm."
I did it, putting the article into the form of a parody on the "Burial of Sir John Moore"—and a pretty crude parody it was, too.

(Passage taken from gutenberg.org)

Detail

1. How did some people pay for their subscription to the paper?

    A. through writing
    B. with work
    C. with vegetables
    D. It was free

Vocabulary

2. What does the word *judiciously* mean?

    A. viciously
    B. with good judgment
    C. on time
    D. jokingly

Cause and Effect

3. What happened as a result of Higgins plans to drown himself?

    A. Higgins died.
    B. A passerby rescued him.
    C. The young Mark Twain wrote an article making fun of him.
    D. The young Mark Twain saw Higgins leave town.

Author's Purpose

4. What was the author's purpose in writing this piece?

    A. To inform
    B. To entertain
    C. To persuade
    D. To contradict

Passage 5

Editorial Wild Oats by Mark Twain

Answer Key

Answers and Explanations

Detail

1. How did some people pay for their subscription to the paper?

C. with vegetables

This is a detail question. Read through the passage to find this detail.

"My uncle had me on his paper (the *Weekly Hannibal Journal*, two dollars a year, in advance—five hundred subscribers, and they paid in cord-wood, cabbages, and unmarketable turnips)…"

Vocabulary

2. What does the word *judiciously* mean?

B. with good judgment

This is a vocabulary question. Read the sentences around the word "judiciously" to figure out its meaning.

"…on a lucky summer's day he left town to be gone a week, and asked me if I thought I could edit one issue of the paper judiciously. Ah! didn't I want to try!"

Cause and Effect

3. What happened as a result of Higgins plans to drown himself?

C. The young Mark Twain wrote an article making fun of him.

This is a cause and effect question where you need to find the result of Higgins actions. The young Mark Twain had pictures of Higgins attempt to drown himself, wrote an article about it, and published it.

"I wrote an elaborately wretched account of the whole matter, and then illustrated it with villainous cuts engraved on the bottoms of wooden type with a jack-knife—one of them a picture of Higgins wading out into the creek in his shirt, with a lantern, sounding the depth of the water with a walking-stick. I thought it was desperately funny and was densely unconscious that there was any moral obliquity about such a publication."

Author's Purpose

4. What was the author's purpose in writing this piece?

B. To entertain

The author's purpose in writing this piece is to entertain. The story tells of Mark Twain's adventures as a young writer.

Passage 6

Folklore

"THE SUN AND THE MOON"

There were once ten brothers who hunted together, and at night they occupied the same lodge. One day, after they had been hunting, coming home they found sitting inside the lodge near the door a beautiful woman. She appeared to be a stranger and was so lovely that all the hunters loved her, and as she could only be the wife of one, they agreed that he should have her who was most successful in the next day's hunt. Accordingly, the next day, they each took different ways, and hunted till the sun went down, when they met at the lodge. Nine of the hunters had found nothing, but the youngest brought home a deer, so the woman was given to him for his wife.

The hunter had not been married more than a year when he was seized with sickness and died. Then the next brother took the girl for his wife. Shortly after he died also, and the woman married the next brother. In a short time, all the brothers died save the eldest, and he married the girl. She did not, however, love him, for he was of a churlish disposition, and one day it came into the woman's head that she would leave him and see what fortune she would meet with in the world. So, she went, taking only a dog with her, and travelled all day. She went on and on, but towards evening she heard some one coming after her who, she imagined, must be her husband. In great fear she knew not which way to turn, when she perceived a hole in the ground before her. There she thought she might hide herself, and entering it with her dog she suddenly found herself going lower and lower, until she passed through the earth and came up on the other side. Near to her there was a lake, and a man fishing in it.

"My grandfather," cried the woman, "I am pursued by a spirit."

"Leave me," cried Manabozho, for it was he, "leave me. Let me be quiet."

The woman still begged him to protect her, and Manabozho at length said—

"Go that way, and you shall be safe."

Hardly had she disappeared when the husband, who had discovered the hole by which his wife had descended, came on the scene.

"Tell me," said he to Manabozho, "where has the woman gone?"

"Leave me," cried Manabozho, "don't trouble me."

"Tell me," said the man, "where is the woman?" Manabozho was silent, and the husband, at last getting angry, abused him with all his might.

"The woman went that way," said Manabozho at last. "Run after her, but you shall never catch her, and you shall be called Gizhigooke (day sun), and the woman shall be called Tibikgizis (night sun)."

So the man went on running after his wife to the west, but he has never caught her, and he pursues her to this day.

(Passage taken from gutenberg.org)

Detail

1. How did the brothers decide which one would get to marry the woman?

A. The most handsome one would get to marry her.
B. The one that she liked the best would marry her.
C. The one who won the hunting contest would marry her.
D. The firstborn son would marry her.

Vocabulary

2. What does the word *eldest* mean?

A. Meanest
B. Oldest
C. Youngest
D. Thinnest

Sequence

3. Which brother was the last one that the woman married?

A. The youngest
B. The oldest
C. The second son
D. The third son

Cause and Effect

4. What was the reason that the woman ran away from the last husband she had?

A. She was afraid of him.
B. He had forced her to leave.
C. She did not love him.
D. He had frightened her.

Passage 6

Folklore

"The Sun and the Moon"

Answer Key

Answers and Explanations

Detail

1. How did the brothers decide which one would get to marry the woman?

C. The one who won the hunting contest would marry her.

This is a detail question. To find the answer, skim through the passage looking for the section that talks about how it was decided who would marry the woman.

"She appeared to be a stranger, and was so lovely that all the hunters loved her, and as she could only be the wife of one, they agreed that he should have her who was most successful in the next day's hunt."

Vocabulary

2. What does the word *eldest* mean?

B. Oldest

This is a vocabulary question. To find the answer, look for the word "eldest" in the passage. Read the sentences around the word "eldest" to use context clues to figure out the meaning.

"Nine of the hunters had found nothing, but the youngest brought home a deer, so the woman was given to him for his wife.

The hunter had not been married more than a year when he was seized with sickness and died. Then the next brother took the girl for his wife. Shortly after he died also, and the woman married the next brother. In a short time all the brothers died save the eldest, and he married the girl."

The sentences reveal that the girl married the youngest brother first and then the next brother until only the eldest was left. This is enough of a clue to realize that he is the oldest of the brothers.

Sequence

3. Which brother was the last one that the woman married?

B. The oldest

222

This is a sequence question. To find the answer, carefully read through the text to figure out the order of events, and you will find that the oldest brother was the last one that the woman married.

Cause and Effect

4. What was the reason that the woman ran away from the last husband she had?

C. She did not love him.

This is a cause and effect question. The answer can be found in the passage where it explains why the woman left the last husband.

"She did not, however, love him, for he was of a churlish disposition, and one day it came into the woman's head that she would leave him and see what fortune she would meet with in the world."

Passage 7

Frankenstein's Creation
By Mary Wollstonecraft Shelley

It was on a dreary night of November that I beheld the accomplishment of my toil. With an anxiety that amounted to agony, I collected the instruments of life around me that I might infuse a spark of being into the lifeless thing that lay at my feet. I saw the dull yellow eye of the creature open; it breathed hard; and a convulsive motion agitated its limbs.

How can I delineate the wretch whom with such infinite pains and care I had endeavoured to form? His yellow skin scarcely covered the work of muscles and arteries beneath; his hair was of a lustrous black, and flowing; his teeth of a pearly whiteness; but his watery eyes seemed almost of the same colour as the dun-white sockets in which they were set.

I had worked hard for nearly two years for the sole purpose of infusing life into an inanimate body. For this I had deprived myself of rest and health. But now that I had finished, breathless horror and disgust filled my heart. Unable to endure the aspect of the being I had created, I rushed out of the room. I tried to sleep, but disturbed by the wildest dreams, I started up. By the dim and yellow light of the moon I beheld the miserable monster whom I had created. He held up the curtains of the bed, and his eyes were fixed on me. He might have spoken, but I did not hear; one hand was stretched out, seemingly to detain me, but I escaped and rushed downstairs.

No mortal could support the horror of that countenance. I had gazed on him while unfinished; he was ugly then, but when those muscles and joints were rendered capable of motion, no mummy could be so hideous. I took refuge in the court-yard and passed the night wretchedly.

(Passage taken from gutenberg.org)

Main Idea

1. What was the main idea of this passage?

A. The creature had yellow skin and yellow eyes.
B. The creature's creator had regret for creating him.
C. The creature's creator was proud of his creation.
D. The creature was ugly but intelligent.

Detail

2. How long did it take to make the creature?

A. One night
B. The whole month of November
C. Almost 2 years
D. 5 years

Vocabulary

3. What does *countenance* mean?

A. numbers
B. facial appearance
C. monster
D. man

Author's Purpose

4. What was the author's purpose in writing this piece?

A. To inform
B. To entertain
C. To persuade
D. To contradict

Passage 7

Frankenstein's Creation

By Mary Wollstonecraft Shelley

Answer Key

Answers and Explanations

Main Idea

1. What was the main idea of this passage?

B. The creature's creator had regret for creating him.

This is a main idea question. The main idea is found within the passage. In various points, the author hints at his regret for creating the creature.

"I had worked hard for nearly two years for the sole purpose of infusing life into an inanimate body. For this I had deprived myself of rest and health. But now that I had finished, breathless horror and disgust filled my heart."

Detail

2. How long did it take to make the creature?

C. Almost 2 years

This is a detail question so you need to skim through the passage for the detail of how long it took to make the creature.

"I had worked hard for nearly two years for the sole purpose of infusing life into an inanimate body."

Vocabulary

3. What does *countenance* mean?

B. facial appearance

This is a vocabulary question. You need to look for the word "countenance" in the passage and read the sentences around it for context clues. The sentences talk about looking at the creature and noticing he was ugly so countenance refers to facial appearance.

"No mortal could support the horror of that countenance. I had gazed on him while unfinished; he was ugly then."

Author's Purpose

4. What was the author's purpose in writing this piece?

B.   To entertain

This is a fictional piece. The only purpose is to entertain the reader with an interesting story.

Passage 8

The Life, Crime and Capture of John Wilkes Booth

By George Alfred Townsend

The curtain had arisen on the third act, *Mrs. Mountchessington* and *Asa Trenchard* were exchanging vivacious stupidities, when a young man, so precisely resembling the one described as J. Wilkes Booth that be is asserted to be the same, appeared before the open door of the President's box, and prepared to enter. The servant who attended Mr. Lincoln said politely, "this is the President's box, sir, no one is permitted to enter." "I am a senator," responded the person, "Mr. Lincoln has sent for me." The attendant gave way, and the young man passed into the box.

As he appeared at the door, taking a quick, comprehensive glance at the interior, Major Rathbone arose. "Are you aware, sir," he said, courteously, "upon whom you are intruding? This is the President's box, and no one is admitted." The intruder answered not a word. Fastening his eyes upon Mr. Lincoln, who had half turned his head to ascertain what caused the disturbance, he stepped quickly back without the door.

Without this door there was an eyehole, bored it is presumed on the afternoon of the crime, while the theater was deserted by all, save a few mechanics. Glancing through this orifice, John Wilkes Booth espied in a moment the precise position of the President; he wore upon his wrinkling face the pleasant embryo of an honest smile, forgetting in the mimic scene the splendid successes of our arms for which he was responsible, and the history he had filled so well.

The cheerful interior was lost to J. Wilkes Booth. He did not catch the spirit of the delighted audience, of the flaming lamps flinging illumination upon the domestic foreground and the gaily-set stage. He only cast one furtive glance upon the man he was to slay, and thrusting one hand in his bosom, another in his skirt pocket, drew forth simultaneously his deadly weapons. His right palm grasped a Derringer pistol, his left a dirk.

Then, at a stride, he passed the threshold again, leveled his arm at the President and bent the trigger.

A keen quick report and a puff of white smoke,—a close smell of powder and the rush of a dark, imperfectly outlined figure,—and the President's head dropped upon his shoulders: the ball was in his brain.

(Passage taken from gutenberg.org)

Detail

1. Who killed Abraham Lincoln?

    A. Rathbone
    B. Derringer
    C. Booth
    D. Trenchard

Vocabulary

2. What does the word *orifice* mean?

    A. doorway
    B. small opening
    C. binoculars
    D. eyeglasses

Inference

3. What did the author mean when he said, "the ball was in his brain"?

    A. John Wilkes Booth has mental problems.
    B. Lincoln had been shot in the head.
    C. Lincoln had a great love of baseball.
    D. John Wilkes Booth was not thinking clearly.

Cause and Effect

4. How did the killer get access to Lincoln's box in the theater?

    A. He lied and said he was a senator.
    B. He threatened security with a gun.
    C. He pretended to be an actor in the play.
    D. He bought a ticket for a seat in Lincoln's box.

Passage 8

The Life, Crime and Capture of John Wilkes Booth

Answer Key

Answers and Explanations

Detail

1. Who killed Abraham Lincoln?

C. Booth

The question is a detail question. Read the passage looking for the detail of who killed Lincoln.

"The cheerful interior was lost to J. Wilkes Booth. He did not catch the spirit of the delighted audience, of the flaming lamps flinging illumination upon the domestic foreground and the gaily-set stage. He only cast one furtive glance upon the man he was to slay, and thrusting one hand in his bosom, another in his skirt pocket, drew forth simultaneously his deadly weapons. His right palm grasped a Derringer pistol, his left a dirk."

Vocabulary

2. What does the word *orifice* mean?

B. small opening

This is a vocabulary question. Look for the word "orifice" in the passage and read the words around it for context clues. The sentence shows that an orifice is a small opening through which Booth looked at Lincoln.

"Glancing through this orifice, John Wilkes Booth espied in a moment the precise position of the President;"

Inference

3. What did the author mean when he said, "the ball was in his brain"?

B. Lincoln had been shot in the head.

The question is an inference question requiring reading the passage and making a conclusion on its meaning. The passage mentioned that Booth bend the trigger, a puff of white smoke, a close smell of powder, and the ball was in his brain.

"Then, at a stride, he passed the threshold again, leveled his arm at the President and bent the trigger.

A keen quick report and a puff of white smoke,—a close smell of powder and the rush of a dark, imperfectly outlined figure,—and the President's head dropped upon his shoulders: the ball was in his brain."

Cause and Effect

4. How did the killer get access to Lincoln's box in the theater?

A.   He lied and said he was a senator.

This question is a cause and effect question. You need to figure out how Booth got into Lincoln's box in the theater.

"The servant who attended Mr. Lincoln said politely, 'this is the President's box, sir, no one is permitted to enter.' 'I am a senator,' responded the person, 'Mr. Lincoln has sent for me.' "

Passage 9

Love Letters of Nathaniel Hawthorne   To Miss Peabody

Brook Farm,

May 4th, 1841.

½ past 1 P.M.

Belovedest, as Mr. Ripley is going to the city this afternoon, I cannot but write a letter to thee, though I have but little time; for the cornfield will need me very soon. My cold no longer troubles me; and all this morning, I have been at work under the clear blue sky, on a hillside. Sometimes it almost seemed as if I were at work in the sky itself; though the material in which I wrought was the ore from our gold mine. Nevertheless, there is nothing so unseemly and disagreeable in this sort of toil, as thou wouldst think. It defiles the hands, indeed, but not the soul. This gold ore is a pure and wholesome substance; else our Mother Nature would not devour it so readily, and derive so much nourishment from it, and return such a rich abundance of good grain and roots in requital of it.

The farm is growing very beautiful now—not that we yet see anything of the peas or potatoes, which we have planted; but the grass blushes green on the slopes and hollows. I wrote that word blush almost unconsciously; so, we will let it go as an inspired utterance. When I go forth afield, I think of my Dove, and look beneath the stone walls, where the verdure is richest, in hopes that a little company of violets, or some solitary bud, prophetic of the summer, may be there; to which I should award the blissful fate of being treasured for a time in thy bosom; for I doubt not, dearest, that thou wouldst admit any flowers of thy husband's gathering into that sweetest place. But not a wildflower have I yet found. One of the boys gathered some yellow cowslips, last Sunday; but I am well content not to have found them; for they are not precisely what I should like to send my Dove, though they deserve honor and praise, because they come to us when no others will. We have our parlor here dressed in evergreen, as at Christmas. That beautifullest little flower vase of thine stands on Mr. Ripley's study table, at which I am now writing. It contains some daffodils and some willow blossoms. I brought it here, rather than kept it in my chamber, because I never sit there, and it gives me many pleasant emotions to look round and be surprised (for it is often a surprise, though I well know that it is there) by something which is connected with the idea of thee.

Most dear wife, I cannot hope that thou art yet entirely recovered from that terrible influenza; but if thou art not almost well, I know not how thy husband will endure it. And that cough too. It is the only one of thy utterances, so far as I have heard them, which I do not love. Wilt thou not be very well, and very lightsome, at our next meeting. I promise myself to be with thee next Thursday, the day after tomorrow. It is an eternity since we met; and I can nowise account for my enduring this lengthened absence so well. I do not believe that I could suffer it, if I were not engaged in a righteous and heaven-blessed way of life. When I was in the Custom-House, and then at Salem, I was not half so patient; though my love of thee has grown infinitely since then.

We had some tableaux last evening, the principal characters being sustained by Mr. Farley and Miss Ellen Slade. They went off very well. I would like to see a tableaux arranged by my Dove.

Dearest, I fear it is time for thy clod-compelling husband to take the field again. Good-bye.

Miss Sophia A. Peabody,
13 West Street,
Boston.

(Passage taken from gutenberg.org)

Main Idea

1. Why did the letter writer write the letter?

    A. To remind his wife of his love for her and to tell her about his work.
    B. To remind her to take care of her health condition.
    C. To let his wife know about his own sickness.
    D. To arrange a meeting between Mr. Ripley and his wife.

Detail

2. What type of work is the letter writer doing?

    A. construction
    B. astronomy
    C. farming
    D. florist

Vocabulary

3. What does the word *utterance* mean?

    A. unconscious
    B. praise
    C. disgust
    D. spoken word or sound

Author's Tone

4. What is the author's tone in this piece?

    A. curious
    B. condescending
    C. affectionate
    D. arrogant

<u>Passage 9</u>

Love Letters of Nathaniel Hawthorne

To MISS PEABODY

Answer Key

Answers and Explanations

Main Idea

1. Why did the letter writer write the letter?

A.   To remind his wife of his love for her and to tell her about his work.

This is a main idea question. The entire passage needed to be read to see why he wrote the letter. For the majority of his letter, the letter writer writes about his work as a farmer and reminds his wife how much he loves her.

Detail

2. What type of work is the letter writer doing?

C.   farming

This is a detail question. There are a few examples in the passage that show the letter writer is a farmer.

Here are a few examples:

"I cannot but write a letter to thee, though I have but little time; for the cornfield will need me very soon.

The farm is growing very beautiful now—not that we yet see anything of the peas or potatoes, which we have planted;"

Vocabulary

3. What does the word *utterance* mean?

D. spoken word or sound

This is a vocabulary question. Look for the word "utterance" and read the surrounding sentences for context clues.

"The farm is growing very beautiful now—not that we yet see anything of the peas or potatoes, which we have planted; but the grass blushes green on the slopes and hollows. I wrote that word blush almost unconsciously; so we will let it go as an inspired utterance."

Author's Tone

4. What is the author's tone in this piece?

C. affectionate

This is a question on author's tone. There are examples of how his letter is affectionate. He calls his loved one, "belovedest".

"Belovedest, as Mr. Ripley is going to the city this afternoon, I cannot but write a letter to thee, though I have but little time;"

He also speaks of his growing love for her.

"When I was in the Custom-House, and then at Salem, I was not half so patient; though my love of thee has grown infinitely since then."

Passage 10

NATURE by Ralph Waldo Emerson

CHAPTER I

To go into solitude, a man needs to retire as much from his chamber as from society. I am not solitary whilst I read and write, though nobody is with me. But if a man would be alone, let him look at the stars. The rays that come from those heavenly worlds, will separate between him and what he touches. One might think the atmosphere was made transparent with this design, to give man, in the heavenly bodies, the perpetual presence of the sublime. Seen in the streets of cities, how great they are! If the stars should appear one night in a thousand years, how would men believe and adore; and preserve for many generations the remembrance of the city of God, which had been shown! But every night come out these envoys of beauty, and light the universe with their admonishing smile.

The stars awaken a certain reverence, because though always present, they are inaccessible; but all natural objects make a kindred impression, when the mind is open to their influence. Nature never wears a mean appearance. Neither does the wisest man extort her secret and lose his curiosity by finding out all her perfection. Nature never became a toy to a wise spirit. The flowers, the animals, the mountains, reflected the wisdom of his best hour, as much as they had delighted the simplicity of his childhood.

(Passage taken from gutenberg.org)

Detail

1. "Nature never wears a mean appearance. Neither does the wisest man extort her secret, and lose his curiosity by finding out all her perfection."

What does this quote mean?

    A. Man tries to harm nature to find out her secrets.
    B. No matter how hard man tries he will never know all the secrets of nature's beauty.
    C. Man is always happy in nature.
    D. Man does not show curiosity about nature.

Vocabulary

2. What does *solitude* mean?

    A. Attitude
    B. Alone
    C. Darkness
    D. Solution

Author's Tone

3. What was the author's tone?

    A. Respectful toward nature
    B. Disappointment in aspects of nature
    C. Solemn tone about nature
    D. Sarcastic tone about nature

Author's Purpose

4. What was the author's purpose?

    A. To persuade
    B. To inform
    C. To entertain
    D. To contradict

Passage 10

Nature by Ralph Waldo Emerson

Answer Key

Answers and Explanations

Detail

1. "Nature never wears a mean appearance. Neither does the wisest man extort her secret, and lose his curiosity by finding out all her perfection."

What does this quote mean?

B. No matter how hard man tries he will never know all the secrets of nature's beauty.

This is a detail question. The answer is found by reading through the passage. The answer is within the quote itself.

Vocabulary

2. What does *solitude* mean?

B. Alone

This is a vocabulary question. Read the sentences around the word "solitude" to figure out its meaning. The sentences give the clue that the word means alone.

"To go into solitude, a man needs to retire as much from his chamber as from society. I am not solitary whilst I read and write, though nobody is with me. But if a man would be alone, let him look at the stars."

Author's Tone

3. What was the author's tone?

A.   Respectful toward nature

The author has a tone of great respect for nature, which is seen throughout the passage.

"The stars awaken a certain reverence, because though always present, they are inaccessible; but all natural objects make a kindred impression, when the mind is open to their influence."

Author's Purpose

4. What was the author's purpose?

C. To entertain

The author's purpose is to entertain the reader about the beauty of nature.

Passage 11

A Book of Myths by Jean Lang

PYGMALION

In days when the world was young and when the gods walked on the earth, there reigned over the island of Cyprus a sculptor-king, and king of sculptors, named Pygmalion. In the language of our own day, we should call him "wedded to his art." In woman he only saw the bane of man. Women, he believed, lured men from the paths to which their destiny called them. While man walked alone, he walked free—he had given no "hostages to fortune." Alone, man could live for his art, could combat every danger that beset him, could escape, unhampered, from every pitfall in life. But woman was the ivy that clings to the oak, and throttles the oak in the end. No woman, vowed Pygmalion, should ever hamper him. And so, at length he came to hate women, and, free of heart and mind, his genius wrought such great things that he became a very perfect sculptor. He had one passion, a passion for his art, and that sufficed him. Out of great rough blocks of marble he would hew the most perfect semblance of men and of women, and of everything that seemed to him most beautiful and the most worth preserving.

When we look now at the Venus of Milo, at the Diana of Versailles, and at the Apollo Belvidere in the Vatican, we can imagine what were the greater things that the sculptor of Cyprus freed from the dead blocks of marble. One day as he chipped and chiseled, there came to him, like the rough sketch of a great picture, the semblance of a woman. How it came he knew not. Only he knew that in that great mass of pure white stone there seemed to be imprisoned the exquisite image of a woman, a woman that he must set free. Slowly, gradually, the woman came. Soon he knew that she was the most beautiful thing that his art had ever wrought. All that he had ever thought that a woman *should* be, this woman was. Her form and features were all most perfect, and so perfect were they, that he felt very sure that, had she been a woman indeed, most perfect would have been the soul within. For her he worked as he had never worked before. There came, at last, a day when he felt that another touch would be insult to the exquisite thing he had created. He laid his chisel aside and sat down to gaze at the Perfect Woman. She seemed to gaze back at him. Her parted lips were ready to speak—to smile. Her hands were held out to hold his hands. Then Pygmalion covered his eyes. He, the hater of women, loved a woman—a woman of chilly marble. The women he had scorned were avenged.

(Passage taken from gutenberg.org)

Main Idea

1. What is the main idea of the piece?

    A. Pygmalion idolized women for the entire piece.
    B. Pygmalion despised women throughout the piece.
    C. Pygmalion started out believing he would never love a woman, but ended up loving a sculpture of a woman.
    D. Pygmalion enjoyed visiting museums to see famous statues.

Detail

2. What title was Pygmalion given?

    A. Sculptor-king
    B. Hostage to fortune
    C. Apollo
    D. Cyprus

Vocabulary

3. What does *avenged* mean?

    A. Average
    B. Found revenge
    C. Made of stone
    D. Cold

Inference

4. What does the author mean in referring to Pygmalion, "Women, he believed, lured men from the paths to which their destiny called them"?

    A. Women distracted men from their true purpose in life.
    B. Women helped men to become better people.
    C. Women encouraged men to pursue their interests.
    D. Women wanted to get married more than men did.

Passage 11

Pygmalion

Answer Key

Answers and Explanations

Main Idea

1. What is the main idea of the piece?

C. Pygmalion started out believing he would never love a woman but ended up loving a sculpture of a woman.

This is a main idea question. The answer is found by reading through the entire piece.

"In woman he only saw the bane of man. Women, he believed, lured men from the paths to which their destiny called them. While man walked alone, he walked free—he had given no 'hostages to fortune.' "

At the end of the piece,

"Then Pygmalion covered his eyes. He, the hater of women, loved a woman—a woman of chilly marble."

Detail

2. What title was Pygmalion given?

A. Sculptor-king

This is a detail question. The answer is found in the beginning of the passage.

"In days when the world was young and when the gods walked on the earth, there reigned over the island of Cyprus a sculptor-king, and king of sculptors, named Pygmalion."

Vocabulary

3. What does *avenged* mean?

B. found revenge

This is a vocabulary question. Read the sentences around the word "avenged" to figure out its meaning.

"Then Pygmalion covered his eyes. He, the hater of women, loved a woman—a woman of chilly marble. The women he had scorned were avenged."

Inference

4. What does the author mean in referring to Pygmalion, "Women, he believed, lured men from the paths to which their destiny called them"?

A. Women distracted men from their true purpose in life.

This is an inference question. The answer can be found by reading the passage and coming to a conclusion from the given information.

"Women, he believed, lured men from the paths to which their destiny called them. While man walked alone, he walked free—he had given no "hostages to fortune." Alone, man could live for his art, could combat every danger that beset him, could escape, unhampered, from every pitfall in life. But woman was the ivy that clings to the oak, and throttles the oak in the end. No woman, vowed Pygmalion, should ever hamper him."

Passage 12

Twilight Stories by Various Authors

"Dixie" and "Yankee Doodle"

I was born 'way down in "Dixie,"
      Reared beneath the Southern skies,
 And they didn't have to teach me
      Every "Yankee" to despise.

I was but a country youngster
      When I donned a suit of gray,
 When I shouldered my old musket,
      And marched forth the "Yanks" to slay.

Four long years I fought and suffered,
      "Dixie" was my battle cry;
 "Dixie" always and forever,
      Down in "Dixie" let me die.

And to-night I'm down in "Dixie"
      "Dixie" still so grand and true;
 But to-night I am appareled
      In a uniform of blue.

And to-night the band is playing;
      'Tis not "Dixie's" strains I hear,
 But the strains of "Yankee Doodle"
      Ring out strong and clear.

Long I listen to the music;
      By my side a comrade stands;
 He's a "Yank" and I'm a "Rebel,"
      But we grasp each other's hands.

Here together we united
      'Way down South in "Dixie" stand,
 And my comrade whispers softly,
      "There's no land like 'Dixie's land.'"

But my eyes are filled with teardrops,
      Tears that make my heart feel glad;
 And I whisper to my comrade:
      " 'Yankee Doodle' ain't so bad."
                 Lawrence Porcher Hext

(Passage taken from gutenberg.org)

Detail

1. How long did the war last?

    A. The poem does not mention how long the war lasted
    B. Two years
    C. Three years
    D. Four years

Vocabulary

2. What is the opposite of the word *despise*?

    A. Hate
    B. Love
    C. Confront
    D. Admire

Inference

3. How did the Southerner's opinion of the "Yankee" change by the end of the poem?

    A. He started to view him as being on his side and not as an enemy
    B. He began to feel jealous of him
    C. He did not change his opinion of him
    D. He started to ignore him

Author's Purpose

4. Which of these is the most important message the author conveys in this piece?

    A. The Southerner wore different colors from the beginning to the end.
    B. The end of the war brought more anger to both the North and the South.
    C. The Southerner was taught to hate Northerners as a child, but he overcame his hatred.
    D. A new war would ensue.

Passage 12

Twilight Stories by Various Authors
Answer Key

Answers and Explanations

Detail

1. How long did the war last?

D. Four years

This is a detail question. Skim through the passage looking for this detail. The answer is found in the line,

"Four long years I fought and suffered."

Vocabulary

2. What is the opposite of the word *despise*?

B. Love

The answer is found in the lines surrounding the word *despise*.

"I was born way down in 'Dixie,'
        Reared beneath the Southern skies,
    And they didn't have to teach me
        Every 'Yankee' to despise.

I was but a country youngster
        When I donned a suit of gray,
    When I shouldered my old musket,
        And marched forth the 'Yanks' to slay."

This is a vocabulary question, and it was essential to read the lines around the word "despise" to figure out its meaning.
These lines explain how he was raised to despise the "Yankee" and put on his uniform, carried his weapon and marched on to kill the "Yankee".

Inference

3. How did the southerner's opinion of the "Yankee" change by the end of the poem?

A. He started to view him as being on his side and not as an enemy.

This is an inference question where you need to read between the lines to figure out the answer.

"Long I listen to the music;
      By my side a comrade stands;
  He's a 'Yank' and I'm a 'Rebel,'
      But we grasp each other's hands.

Here together we united
      'Way down South in 'Dixie' stand,
  And my comrade whispers softly,
      "There's no land like 'Dixie's land'.

But my eyes are filled with teardrops,
      Tears that make my heart feel glad;
  And I whisper to my comrade:
      'Yankee Doodle' ain't so bad.' "

These lines show how the Southerner changed his opinion of the "Yankee" by being united in holding hands and appreciating the Northern song "Yankee Doodle".

Author's Purpose

4. Which of these is the most important message the author conveys in this piece?

C. The Southerner was taught to hate Northerners as a child, but he overcame his hatred.

The author of the passage shows the feelings of the Southerner toward Northerners from the beginning to end. The overcoming of his hatred is the most important message in the passage.

Made in United States
Orlando, FL
04 April 2022

16472022R00137